Problem Regions of Europe
General Editor: **D. I. Scargill**

The Mezzogiorno
Alan B. Mountjoy

OXFORD UNIVERSITY PRESS

Oxford University Press, Walton Street, Oxford OX2 6DP

Oxford London Glasgow New York
Toronto Melbourne Wellington Cape Town
Nairobi Dar es Salaam Kuala Lumpur
Singapore Jakarta Hong Kong Tokyo Delhi
Bombay Calcutta Madras Karachi

© Oxford University Press 1973

First published 1973
Reprinted 1974, 1978 (with revision), and 1979

Filmset by BAS Printers Limited, Over Wallop, Hampshire
and printed in Great Britain
at the University Press, Oxford
by Eric Buckley, Printer to the University

Editor's Preface

Great economic and social changes have taken place in Europe in recent years. The agricultural labour force has almost everywhere contracted, in some places very rapidly, and the lack of alternative forms of employment in rural areas has resulted in large-scale movements of farmers and farm labourers in search of work in the cities. The scale of this drift from the land can be gauged from the fact that in the six (original) Common Market countries the agricultural work force was halved between 1950 and 1970: from approximately 20 millions to 10 millions. In many areas this rural exodus has made it possible to carry out much needed reorganization of farm holdings, but it has also brought with it problems concerning, for example, the provision of services to a contracting population and the need to establish new forms of land use where farming is no longer profitable.

Contraction of the labour force has also taken place in several old-established industries. These include coal-mining, shipbuilding, and the more traditional textile industries, where the effects of a shrinking market have been made more severe by automation, which has substituted machines for men. The coal-mining industry of Western Europe shed something like two-thirds of its labour force during the 1950s and 1960s. Wherever a large proportion of the working population was dependent upon a declining industry of this kind, the problems of adjustment have been severe. Many schemes have been devised to attract alternative forms of employment but, despite incentives, it has often proved difficult to attract new firms because of the old industrial areas' legacy of dirt, derelict landscape, poor housing, and, in some places, bad labour relations.

Problems of a different kind have arisen as a result of the continued growth of large cities such as London and Paris, or of groups of closely related cities as in the case of Randstad Holland. The reasons for such growth are several. To the manufacturer the big city offers the advantage of a local market, a varied labour force, and easy access to suppliers and other manufacturers with whom he needs to maintain close links. To them and even more to the service industries a city location offers a prestige location, and the enormous expansion of service activity, especially office-work, has contributed greatly to postwar urban growth. Attempts to control the increase of employment within cities have had some success as far as manufacturing industry is concerned but very little with regard to office work.

Problems resulting from city growth include traffic congestion, high land prices, pollution, and social stress brought about by factors such as housing shortages and travelling long distances to work. Yet the city continues to attract migrants for whom the image is still one of streets paved with gold, whilst the established resident is loath to leave the 'bright lights', the football club, or the familiar shops.

Geographers, in the past, have been reluctant to focus their attention on regional problems. The problem was thought to be a temporary phenomenon and therefore less worthy of consideration than regional characteristics of a more enduring nature—the landscape or the chimerical *personality* of the region. Yet such is the magnitude, persistence, and areal extent of problems of the kind referred to above that the geographer would seem to be well justified in approaching his regional study by seeking to identify, measure, and even seek solutions to problems.

'Devenant alors un cadre de recherche, la région sera choisie en fonction de certains problèmes et des moyens qui permettent de les aborder avec profit' (H. Baulig). Indeed it has been suggested that regions can be defined in terms of the problems with which they are confronted.

Additional stimulus for studying regional problems arises from the interest which politicians and planners have recently shown in the region as a framework for tackling such issues as the relief of unemployment, the siting of new investment, and the reorganization of administrative boundaries. Governments have long been aware of the problems resulting from economic and social changes and various attempts have been made to solve them. Development Areas and New Towns in Great Britain, for example, represent an attempt to deal with the problems, on the one hand, of the declining industrial areas and, on the other, of the overgrown cities. Such solutions can hardly be described as regional, however. Other countries have recognized the problems of their over-populated rural areas and the Cassa per il

3

Mezzogiorno, the Fund for the South, was set up by the Italian government in 1950 in order to encourage investment in the South. The E.E.C. has also channelled funds via its Investment Bank, both to southern Italy and to other parts of the Common Market distant from the main centres of economic activity. Planning of this kind shows an awareness of the regional extent of economic and social problems, though in practice much of the actual work of planning was undertaken on a piecemeal, local, and short-term basis.

Since about 1960, however, the continuing nature of the problems has persuaded most European governments to adopt longer-term and more comprehensive planning measures, and the importance of seeking regional solutions has been increasingly stressed. The last ten years have, in fact, witnessed the setting up of regional planning authorities in many European countries and to them has been given the task of identifying regional problems and of finding solutions to them. A large number of reports have been published following research carried out by these authorities, and individual governments have introduced regional considerations to national planning. The French *métropoles d'équilibre*, for example, were devised in order to introduce new vigour to the regions via the largest provincial towns.

One of the drawbacks to regional planning of this kind is the outdated nature of local government boundaries, most planning decisions having to be implemented through a system of local government more suited to nineteenth than to late twentieth century conditions. Some experts have thus advocated a regional alternative to existing local government areas, and it is interesting to note that the Royal Commission on Local Government in England (the Maud Report), whilst not supporting so radical a change, nevertheless introduced the idea of *provinces* within which broad planning policies could be carried out. Supporters of the regional idea argue that a growing trend toward State centralization is bringing about a reaction in the form of renewed popular interest in regions, their history, industrial archaeology, customs, dialect, and so on.

The revival of interest in regions, both for their own sake and as a practical aid to planning or administration, makes particularly timely the appearance of a series of geographical studies concerned with *Problem Regions of Europe*. The present volume is one of 12 studies comprising such a series.

The twelve regions have been selected in order to illustrate, between them, a variety of problems. The most obvious of these are: problems of a harsh environment, of isolation, of industrial decay, of urban congestion, and of proximity to a sensitive political frontier. One or other of these major problems forms the dominant theme in each of the volumes of the series, but they have not been studied in isolation. Where it has been thought relevant to do so, authors have drawn attention to similar problems encountered in other parts of the continent so that readers may compare both the causes of problems and the methods employed to solve them. At the same time it is recognized that every region has a number of problems that are unique to itself and these peculiarly local problems have been distinguished from those of a more general kind.

Although the precise treatment of each subject will vary according to the nature of the region concerned and, to some extent, the outlook of a particular author, readers will find much in common in the arrangement of contents in each volume. In each of them the nature of the problem or problems which characterize the region is first stated by the author; next the circumstances that have given rise to the problems are explained; after this the methods that have been employed to overcome the problems are subjected to critical examination and evaluation. Each study includes indications of likely future developments.

All the authors of the series have considerable first-hand knowledge of the regions about which they have written. Yet none of them would claim to have a complete set of answers to any particular regional problem. For this reason, as well as from a desire to make the series challenging, each volume contains suggestions for further lines of inquiry that the reader may pursue. The series was conceived initially as one that would be helpful to sixth-form geographers but it is believed that individual volumes will also provide a useful introduction to the detailed work undertaken by more advanced students both of geography and of European studies in general.

D.I.S.

St. Edmund Hall,
August 1972

4

Contents

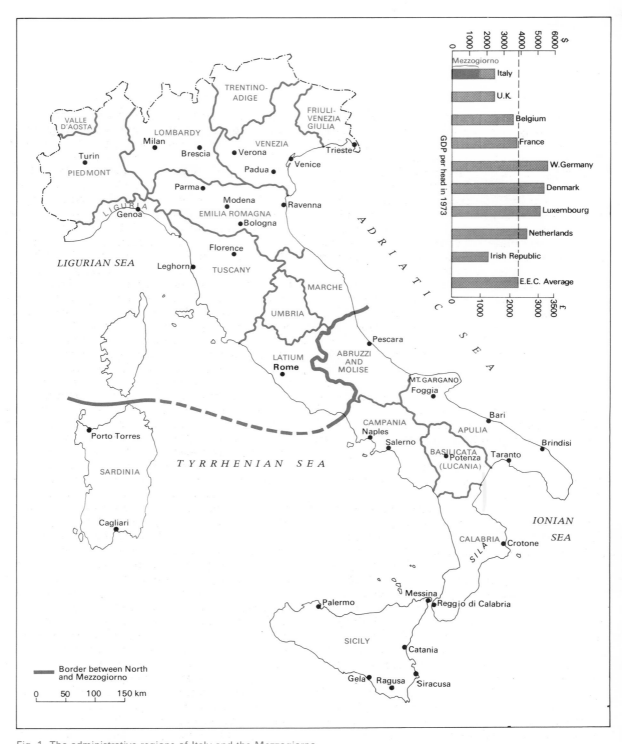

Fig. 1. The administrative regions of Italy and the Mezzogiorno

Introduction

The Mezzogiorno ('midday') conjures up an image of hot, desiccated landscapes somnolent under a torrid midday sun. For a good deal of the year this is true of many parts of southern Italy, and suggests that geographical factors play a significant part in Italy's 'southern problem'. Geographers will recognize that the southern part of the Italian peninsula and the islands of Sicily and Sardinia are truly Mediterranean, whereas the remainder of Italy is not. The disabilities of the Mediterranean type of climate leave their impress on the landscape: the heat and aridity of the summer, the heavy downpours of early winter; but in no sense can the backwardness of the South, its economic under-development, be attributed solely to such factors. One must examine the region in time as well as space and note that the South has been a poor backward region for a very long time, that its economy stagnated and thus has become out-distanced by the modernized forward-pushing economy of Italy's North. The great centres of Italian industry, banking, and commerce are in the North, where also have been found the dynamic elements of national life. The South, still mainly agricultural, has been subjected to the difficulties of terrain, climate, and its history. It has remained backward and poor.

Most countries of Western Europe have within their boundaries depressed, or problem, areas but in the case of Italy the economic split exhibits a pronounced regional pattern. The South includes two-fifths of all Italy and nearly two-fifths of its population (20 out of 54 million); its problems can no longer be shrugged off. A new element in the post-war world is the European Economic Community (Common Market), of which Italy is a member. The Mezzogiorno is no longer just Italy's problem, for it is also the most pronounced problem region within the E.E.C. By the Treaty of Rome, which established the Community, member countries are pledged to do all in their power to reduce economic differences between regions and to lessen backwardness. Thus, attempts to grapple with the problems of the Mezzogiorno have received much attention in the post-war world, and a study of Italy's South over the last twenty years is not only of interest to the economic and social geographer, but also to those concerned with other problem regions and their economic development.

The Mezzogiorno is officially defined as including seven out of Italy's nineteen administrative regions: Abruzzi-Molise, Apulia, Basilicata, Campania, Calabria, Sicily, and Sardinia, together with small parts of the region of Latium (Fig 1). Thus the northern boundary of the Mezzogiorno on the Adriatic side of the peninsula is farther north than Rome, although generally the South is regarded as that part of Italy lying to the south of Rome. This large area exhibits considerable diversity of character and is not even homogeneous in its poverty, although in dealing with 'the South' as a unit for economic rehabilitation all too often economic homogeneity tends to be assumed. Within the South itself some of the areas of greatest poverty lie in Sicily and Calabria.

The attempts since 1950 to rehabilitate the Mezzogiorno are of world-wide interest to regional planners. Problems of regional imbalance face all countries, but no satisfactory mechanism for balancing them has yet been devised. The Italian problem is large enough, and has been tackled long enough, for increasingly comprehensive policies to be pursued as related problems have emerged. Formerly government help to depressed areas was of the public works/public assistance variety, which at best was only a palliative. Now it is accepted that measures on purely local terms are ineffective, and that local economies must be fitted into both regional and national frames. Thus have arisen far-reaching regional policies that aim at imposing new direction and character to regional economies by means of massive government investment and interventions, aimed at both pointing and smoothing the way for the private investor, who has a large part to play in completing the picture. These new strategies give a new dimension to the study of regional geography, and their inclusion in the geographer's field of study gives a relevance to the real world that was all too often missing from earlier more stereotyped studies of 'the region'.

1 The South in the Middle of the Twentieth Century

For comparative purposes 1950 is a year that will always be important in the modern development of southern Italy, for it marked the beginning of major moves by the nation as a whole to rehabilitate the poverty-stricken, backward Mezzogiorno. During that year a number of land reform laws were passed and 'Enti di Riforma' (Reform Agencies) set up and, even more important from the point of view of long-term economic development, there was established the 'Cassa per il Mezzogiorno' (Fund for the South), a semi-autonomous government agency to oversee and co-ordinate the South's economic development. The Cassa was first to operate for the decade 1950–60, but subsequent extensions have prolonged its life until 1980.

By 1950 affairs in the South had become critical. Already Italian industrial output equalled its pre-war production, thanks mainly to American Marshall Aid which generously was helping the rebuilding and re-equipping of war-damaged factories, mainly in the North. Aid worth nearly $2,000 million was given. Much of the South had been fought over and could show more scars of war than the North, but its predominantly agricultural economy with a substantial latifundi (or large estates) pattern seemed to respond more slowly to capital aid. Conditions in the South worsened as agriculture stagnated. In the North the stimulus of cheap power from the recently discovered methane gas under the North Italian plain and the display of high entrepreneurial ability in such men of vision as Mattei, Olivetti, and Pirelli, who have become father figures in Italian industry, fashioned an expanding economy with growing industrial employment opportunities.

The South lacked industrial plants and possessed only limited infrastructure: roads, water supply, housing, etc. It could offer only a restricted range of employment, for there was little available outside agriculture. The war had seen a high proportion of southern males drafted into the Italian army and when the war ended they returned home, many from prisoner-of-war internment in other lands. They swelled the ranks of the unemployed, and as poverty and land-hunger increased they became an active element in peasant riots and illegal squatting on latifundi land.

In 1950 the proportion of the working population of the Mezzogiorno engaged in agriculture was officially put at 55 per cent, but if one allows for the low figure of 20 per cent in the province of industrialized and urban Naples (part of the region of Campania), it can be deduced that the proportion over most of the South must have been nearer 70 per cent. In the hilly and mountainous parts (for example the Molise) where agriculture was almost the sole means of livelihood, the figure rose to 80 per cent. Pressure upon agriculture had been increasing since 1930, partly as a result of the active discouragement of emigration by Mussolini's Fascist government. Between 1890 and 1930 emigration had provided a useful safety valve and some seven million southerners had emigrated.

Between 1930 and 1950 numbers employed in agriculture fell in northern Italy but in the South the agricultural labour force actually increased by half a million (a 17 per cent rise). More important, unemployment increased, but mainly in the form of under-employment. Day-labourers (braccianti) found work for only 100–150 days a year and on peasant-owned or rented plots family labour was largely inactive, being employed well beyond the point of diminishing returns. The poor employment opportunities in the South were also demonstrated by the low proportion of 'active' to 'total' population—39 per cent in the South against 46 per cent in the North.

Although the Mezzogiorno is well known for an agricultural structure that emphasizes the latifundi, it is important to realize that small fragmented properties or tenancies present the other side of the coin. This is partly explained by the alternative ways of utilizing land held in large estates: to work the land in one big 'capitalist farm', or to divide it up and lease small plots to a land-hungry peasantry. For the most part large holdings on the plains were worked as large farms with only a small proportion let to share-croppers, and it was the large holdings on poorer hilly and mountainous land that generally became divided among tenants and share-croppers. Much of the land farmed by small owners and share-tenants was of hilly character. Of the cultivated land in the Mezzogiorno 56 per cent is on slopes of more than 15° against 46 per cent in the North. Further, 49 per cent of this land in the South is without drainage systems, compared with 24 per cent in the North. A peasant farmer might own a number of tiny widely-scattered plots supplemented by others rented or cultivated as a share-tenant, and he might also endeavour to find some work as a day labourer for larger farmers. In terms of grain, vegetables, milk, and wool he was mainly self-sufficient and put little into commercial channels.

Pressure of population by 1950 had led to 'pulverization' of holdings, that is to a reduction in size to below two hectares (five acres) accompanied by much fragmentation. Fragmentation affects agriculture all over Italy but it is at its greatest in the South where one-fifth of farmland is cultivated in holdings made up of between five and ten non-contiguous plots. Such a pattern does not favour modern mechanized methods of farming nor facilitate crop specialization and is a symptom of the under-capitalized, labour-intensive methods prevailing in the South in 1950. Returns from such holdings, especially if a proportion was share-cropped, were becoming inadequate to support a family. Tiny holdings and fragmentation perpetuated antiquated, labour-intensive methods of cultivation and retarded investment in the modernization of southern agriculture. Insecurity of land tenure has also had a damaging effect upon agriculture in the South, as well as upon the morale of the peasantry. Application of money and labour to the land is discouraged by complex and temporary tenures and it is noteworthy that in the few areas where dispersed agricultural settlement prospers (e.g. the *trulli* zone—houses with distinctive conical roofs—in the Salentine peninsula) tenure is secure; thus the peasants have felt it worthwhile to clear the land of stones, to build and keep in repair stone walls around their fields, and to create a farming landscape of orderly prosperity.[1]

The low productivity of the Mezzogiorno is revealed when assessments are made of the distribution of the national income by regions. With nearly two-fifths of the total population of Italy, in the early 1950s the South contributed only about one-fifth of the gross national product. The economic structure of the South was characterized by the predominance of the agricultural sector which demonstrated fluctuation of output from year to year. Further, agriculture in Italy has a lower productivity than industry and both agriculture and industry in the South have a lower level of productivity than in the North.

Estimates of income per head can provide only a rough guide to regional disparities for, in particular, it is not easy to evaluate in monetary terms the subsistence element in southern farming and, of course, overall figures can mask quite severe local differences. Nevertheless, the published figure of net income per head for southern Italy at this time was just under £100; that for northern Italy was £220. This gives a tangible indicator both of the relative positions of North and South and also of the marked poverty in the South (net income per head in U.K. in 1951 was about £350). Statistics from the Italian census of 1951 give a stark picture of the economic and social conditions at that time in the Mezzogiorno. It was recorded that 40 per cent of all dwellings in the South were without any sanitary arrangements whatsoever, compared with 16 per cent in the North. No less than 51 per cent of dwelling-houses in the South were without drinking water from either well or main supply, compared with 23 per cent in the North.

If one studies the statistics of accommodation the overcrowded conditions in the South are underlined. The average number of persons per room in occupied dwellings in the South was 1·8 against 1·2 in the North. Expressed as the proportion of population living in houses with more than two persons per room (a better measure to demonstrate overcrowding) the figure was 53 per cent for the South and 19 per cent for the North. Perhaps worst of all, but a revealing glimpse of true conditions, is that nearly 900 000 persons in the Mezzogiorno in 1951 were not living in proper dwellings at all, but in huts, caves, cellars, arches of old walls, and so on. Carlo Levi in his thought-provoking book *Christ Stopped at Eboli*, which was published in 1946, paints a grim picture of the cave dwellings that housed most of the population of Matera until after the war, dwellings that tourists can still visit. These 'houses' were scooped out of the limestone walls of a deep gorge. They boasted brick fronts with simple ornamentation and the roofs of these brick facades provided a roadway for the layer of caves above. In the dark interior, with walls cut out of the rock, 'I saw a few pieces of miserable furniture, beds and some ragged clothes hanging up to dry. On the floor lay dogs, sheep, goats, and pigs. Most families had just one cave to live in and there they all sleep together; men, women, children, and animals. This is how twenty thousand people live.'[2]

1. R. E. Dickinson, 'Land reform in southern Italy', *Economic Geography*, **30**, p. 159 (1954).

2. C. Levi, *Christ Stopped at Eboli*, p. 84, Cassell, London (1948).

An abundance of children characterized the villages and towns of the Mezzogiorno; ragged, sick, ill-kept waifs, a prey to trachoma and other fly-born diseases such as dysentry, to malaria, to rickets, and to general malnutrition. Schooling was uncertain and generally rudimentary, as were the majority of the health services. Professionally trained doctors, veterinary surgeons, and teachers sought to avoid what was tantamount to exile in the poverty-stricken South. In 1951 one-quarter of the population over six years of age in the South was illiterate; in the North it was only one-sixteenth. Levi's accounts of life in a number of villages in the Lucanian Apennines reveal the destitution, wretchedness, and feelings of hopelessness among their inhabitants, a prey to the scourge of malaria and to whom strangers from the North were as visitors from another world.

For too many in the South poverty was extreme and life bitter. The tax-man's account of his day to Carlo Levi paints a picture of pathetic conditions in a tiny hilltop village in the Lucanian Apennines just before the last war. 'Today I came to make seizures. They don't pay their taxes. And when I come to seize their chattels, there's nothing to be had. I went to three houses and there was no furniture in any of them, except for beds, and we can't touch them. I had to be satisfied with a goat and a few pigeons. Most of them here in Gagliano own a bit of land, even if it's two or three hours' walking distance from the village; sometimes, of course, it's poor soil and yields them practically nothing. The taxes are heavy, it's true, but that's not my affair. You know how the peasants are, they claim that every year's a bad one. They're loaded down with debts, they have malaria and they've no food. But I'd be in a pretty fix if I listened to them. Well, they don't pay, and I have to seize what I can lay my hands on, stuff that's quite worthless. Sometimes I come all this way for a few bottles of oil and a little flour. And with that they scowl at me; there is hate in their eyes. Two years ago, at Missanello, they shot at me . . .'[3]. Bread and olives provided the staple diet for a mass of the southern peasantry; meat was a luxury. In the whole of the South in the mid-1950s the average consumption of meat per head per annum was 10 kgm (24 lb); twice as much was consumed per head in the North of Italy and five times as much per head in the United Kingdom.

Although in 1951 the South contained 18 million inhabitants, 38 per cent of the total population

of Italy, it remained remote and neglected. Communications with the South from the go-ahead North and from Rome, the administrative capital, were poor. Twenty years were to pass before wide and fast autostrade pushed right down the peninsula to both 'toe' and 'heel'. In 1951 metalled roads were narrow and bumpy and often extremely circuitous, conforming to the topography and ascending and descending with each hilltop town en route. Much of the railway system was single-track with sharp curves and steep gradients, and rail movement was leisurely. There were few cars to be seen on the network of unsurfaced lanes that served the farming community, instead carts and wagons drawn by mules and oxen provided the main traffic.

Industrial development in the Mezzogiorno was limited in extent, scope, and size. The only real major centre of heavy and manufacturing industry was Naples, the former capital of the Kingdom of the Two Sicilies. The population of the province of Naples in 1951 was over two million. The density of about 1750 persons per square kilometre was the highest in Italy and among the highest in Western Europe. Within the city itself (pop. one million) incredibly high densities and extreme poverty were to be found in some of the older parts. In 1951 nearly 100 000 persons were engaged in manufacturing industry, far ahead of any other centre in the South, but equally, well below that of the major towns in the North (for example, Turin employed three times that number in manufacturing industry). More than mere numbers are required in analysing levels of industry and we find in Naples at this time an industrial structure demonstrating a dual character whereby a few large-scale, modern plants operated amid a vast number of tiny establishments of workshop rather than factory character which mainly employed family labour.

Within the province of Naples 40 per cent of employment in manufacturing industry was within the few large firms, the rest was in the smaller establishments employing ten or fewer workers. The bulk of industry, represented by the smaller undertakings, had no motor power and the efficiency of their operations was low. The larger undertakings were branches of firms established in the North or in Rome and many of them were part of the state-owned I.R.I. complex. The I.R.I. (Istituto per la Ricostruzione Industriale), which now has important interests in the Mezzogiorno, was formed in 1933 to protect the depositors of the large banks which were then in difficulties. It took over from

3. Carlo Levi, *op. cit.*, p. 34.

the banks a wide range of agricultural and industrial assets and, although it was an emergency body designed to function as a liquidator, in 1937 it was converted into a permanent body with the function of State shareholder. It was authorized to acquire new holdings in the public interest either on its own or associated with private capital and, for example, during the war period it joined with Pirelli in the manufacture of synthetic rubber. By 1950 the I.R.I. had disposed of earlier holdings in farming, land, construction, and the textile industry and had come to concentrate upon electricity, telephones, shipping, steel, and engineering concerns. It was then responsible for 50 per cent of Italy's steel output, 25 per cent of electricity produced, and possessed about 20 per cent of Italy's merchant tonnage.

It must not be thought that the larger 'modern' plants were automatically more efficient than the miniscule concerns. In 1950 the I.R.I. plants in Naples were generally inefficiently run and several were in financial difficulties. These larger factories and plants produced iron and steel, machinery and metal products, chemicals, and cotton textiles while the small establishments produced foodstuffs, clothing, wood products, and leather goods. Thus among the small industries especially there

A.B.M.

Much industry in the South is of a small-scale, family character. Here, in the sunshine at Pulsano, south of Taranto, a tarpaulin is being stitched

was a close link with the resources and the needs of agriculture. Away from Naples most industry was of small-scale, artisan character; only in the larger towns such as Bari, Catania, and Palermo

TABLE I

Industrial employment in the Mezzogiorno, 1951

Industries	Thousands employed in Mezzogiorno	Percentage of those employed in all Italy	Percentage employed in small establishments*
Group 1. Large-scale sector			
Manufacturing	138·6	6·6	28·3
Mining	48·7	41·0	14·0
Electricity	14·2	21·1	25·1
Total, Group 1	201·5	8·9	24·7
Group 2. Small-scale sector			
Manufacturing	414·2	29·4	76·2
Water	4·7	39·6	42·4
Gas	1·8	12·7	1·8
Construction	111·5	21·0	15·6
Total, Group 2	532·2	27·1	63·4
Total for Mezzogiorno	733·7	17·3	52·9

*Employing ten or fewer workers.

Source: Adapted from V. Lutz, *Italy: A Study in Economic Development*, p. 94. O.U.P., London (1962).

TABLE 2

Italy: vital population statistics, 1901–70

	Rate per thousand					
	South			*North*		
	Crude birth rate	Crude death rate	Natural increase	Crude birth rate	Crude death rate	Natural increase
1901–10	31·6	21·8	9·8	31·2	20·0	11·2
1911–20	30·7	23·6	7·1	24·1	18·2	5·9
1921–30	31·5	17·8	13·7	27·2	16·5	10·7
1931–40	29·7	16·1	13·6	20·6	12·9	7·7
1941–50	26·0	13·5	12·5	17·3	12·2	5·1
1951–60	23·2	9·0	14·2	14·6	10·0	4·6
1970	17·7	8·4	9·3	14·5	10·4	4·1

were a few factories, olive mills, and fruit-packing plants of any size to be found.

Except for the more recent discoveries of oil and natural gas Italy has lacked substantial mineral deposits and therefore has had only a small mining industry. The only minerals of value to industry mined in the South are large quantities of sulphur in Sicily and small deposits of lead and zinc in Sardinia. The 1951 census shows that nearly 50 000 were employed in mining in the Mezzogiorno or almost one-quarter of total employment in the large-scale sector (Table 1, Group 1). The total in this large-scale sector (201 500) represents only 9 per cent of the national total in this group. On the other hand, in the Group 2 industries, mainly of a smaller scale, there were (excluding construction) some 420 700 employed, or 30 per cent of the national total in this group. In service, or tertiary, employment the South also contrasts unfavourably when set against the North. Seventy-four per cent of those engaged in commerce in Italy were to be found in the North, and consequently the number engaged in commerce per thousand inhabitants was far less in the South than in the North. Similarly in transport and communications, banking, and insurance over 70 per cent of the employment was in the North.[4]

A final factor that has been of great importance in the South is pressure of population. Death-rates in the South have been higher than in the North and until the First World War the rate of natural increase in the South was actually slightly lower than in the North (Table 2), but subsequently this pattern became reversed as northern birth- and death-rates dropped sharply as living standards were raised. Emigration, both overseas and to the North, helped to keep the ratio between the populations of the two areas reasonably constant until the early 1920s. During the first two decades of this century (excluding the war years) the South supplied the larger part of the eight million Italians who emigrated and, although a considerable number subsequently returned home, the relief of population pressure by net migration was substantial. The severe reduction in emigration under the Fascist government between the wars caused a build-up of pressure upon the South's ill-developed resources which, aggravated by the dislocations of the Second World War, came to a head in the rural troubles of the immediate post-war years.

These features drawn widely from social and economic fields demonstrate very clearly the differing levels of economic development in the North and South of Italy in 1950 and emphasize the depressed levels of the South. In the South was to be found the major part of the low-income sector of the national economy reflecting an over-dependence upon under-capitalized agriculture by a population increasing at above the national rate. The poverty which bred distressing and harsh conditions of life for most of the South's population was a reproach to all Italians. Rioting and demonstrations by the peasantry in the years immediately after the war brought home to the government and to the Italian people the urgent realization that the moment had come for massive remedial action that would give a new deal to the South.

4. V. Lutz, *Italy: A Study in Economic Development*, p. 94, O.U.P., London (1962).

2 The Origins of Under-development in the Mezzogiorno

Geographical factors

There is no single cause to which the social and economic under-development of the Mezzogiorno may be attributed; if there were, a solution to the problems of the South might be far easier. Instead we become aware of inadequacies of both physical and social environments that may be traced far back into the past. Thus, for a better understanding of the problems and difficulties of the South we must examine geographical, historical, and social factors.

The geography of the Mezzogiorno has been an important contributive factor to its wavering fortunes over many centuries. In terms of latitude it is not often realized that the southern part of Sicily lies farther south than Tunis and Algiers in north-west Africa. This is the truly Mediterranean part of Italy and in the extreme south—Apulia, Calabria, and Sicily—the summer heat is torrid and of African character and the drought complete. Next, the position within the Mediterranean basin must be noted: this southern part of the Italian peninsula and the island of Sicily occupy a central position and, indeed, divide this inland sea into eastern and western basins. The central position has made this part of Italy a meeting-ground and arena for a series of invaders, colonists, and merchants throughout recorded times. To this central position must be added a highly articulated coastline, derived from dissections that reflect geology and earth movements and demonstrate themselves in promontories and bays, in the configuration of 'toe' and 'heel', and in the islands of Sicily and Sardinia. Such a coastline offered anchorages and harbours to the early seafarers and settlers and later to marauders and invaders.

Much of the terrain of southern Italy and its island appendages is mountainous; extensive plains are confined to limited coastal situations as around Foggia, part of the Salentine peninsula or 'heel' of Italy, and the hinterland of Naples. The mountain range of the Apennines consists of dissected and discontinuous folds embracing valleys and inter-montane basins. In the bare limestone Abruzzi on the northern borders of the Mezzogiorno are Italy's highest peaks: Corno Grande attaining 2915 m with several other peaks nearby surpassing 2400 m. From there, against the Adriatic, the mountain chains sweep southwards to the Pollino massif at the top of Calabria, Italy's 'toe', at the same time swinging towards the Tyrrhenian Sea side of the peninsula. Many of the peaks are from 1200 to 1500 m in height; Pollino itself attains 2275 m. Most of the southern Apennines are composed of limestone and much of it forming the higher areas is dolomitic. On the eastern flank are younger rocks of sandstones and marls while to the west are volcanic areas. Much of Calabria is of crystalline (granitic) rock and much of the 'heel' comprises low limestone plateaux with lower terraces of sandy and clayey marine deposits. Sicily continues the geology of the mainland, with crystalline rocks in the north-east abutting the volcanic massif of Etna and with mainly sandstones, clays, and conglomerates elsewhere. In Sardinia the rocks are generally older than in the peninsula; Palaeozoic rocks outcrop in the south (among them small coal deposits) while crystalline rocks predominate in the north. The limestone area is small.

The character of a country's rocks, in terms of height, steepness of slopes, porosity or impermeability, and the nature of the soil cover, has significant effects upon ways of life and southern Italy has an unfortunate geological endowment. The hard dolomitic limestone offers sharp peaks and steep slopes and, where the limestone is pure, the dry surface supports a mere vestige of soil and plant cover. The softer limestones of Apulia result in low stony tablelands with, locally, karstic conditions. The extensive limestone areas are highly permeable and therefore are almost devoid of surface drainage. The claylands are difficult to work, being heavy and tenacious in the wet winter season and hard, parched, and dusty under the hot summer sun. Hills of conglomerates, young sandstones, and laminated clays weather and erode easily and where the vegetative cover has been removed now exhibit a landscape of raw, bare rock and deeply eroded gulleys. Such an environment offers poor agricultural resources, and this harsh terrain is reinforced by a similarly disadvantageous climate.

Except where altitude accounts for some modification, this part of Italy experiences the true Mediterranean climate. The mean monthly temperature for the hottest month is 24·5–25·5°C (Naples 24·2°C; Siracusa 25·9°C) and for the coldest month about 7°C (Naples 8·2°C; Foggia 6·3°C). Mean monthly figures disguise actual daily readings and in the extreme South and in Sicily by 2 p.m. of a summer's afternoon, temperatures of over 32°C are common and occasionally 38°C (100°F) is surpassed. These temperatures and long hours of sunshine, although uncomfortable for manual labour, do favour a wide range of crops provided that adequate water is also available, but in this lies the South's greatest handicap. Rainfall over southern Italy and the islands is limited in amount and highly seasonal in occurrence. On the west side of the peninsula and along the north coast of Sicily annual precipitation is about 750 mm, but over the rest of the area, especially on the eastern side of the mountains (owing to the swing of the Apennines, a very large area), annual totals as low as 500 mm are recorded. Most of this rainfall occurs in the late autumn and early winter in the form of sharp, short, but heavy, downpours interspersed with fine clear days. The high rate of evaporation, the destructive character of much of the rainfall, and its considerable unreliability from year to year are inimical to most forms of agriculture.

Despite the southerly position, winter in the mountains is bleak. Snow falls on the uplands each winter and on the highest parts, such as on the Abruzzi and the Sila Grande, the snow-cover may remain for three to four months. Frosts, although rare around the coasts, are a normal occurrence in the mountains. Potenza, at 820 m, has an average of forty days of frost a year. Farmers are not concerned with climate so much as with weather, and here sudden hail-storms can ruin crops, autumnal rainstorms sweep away topsoil, and infrequent and un-expected snowfalls destroy delicate fruit trees. There is, indeed, a 'natural poverty' in the South with its small proportion of plain to total area of farmland, its large area of hill and mountain, its steep eroded slopes, its dry stony beds of seasonal streams, its parched and desiccated appearance.

In the long hot summer months with scant rainfall the trees wilt, the grass coarsens, dries up, and even dies. Without irrigation, crops are poor and limited while pastoral activities are mainly restricted to sheep-rearing, especially in the hilly areas where an element of transhumance survives. These harsh natural conditions have placed southern agriculture in a considerably inferior position to agriculture in the North of Italy. Add to this, remoteness from markets and poor transport facilities and we arrive at a position that recognizes the generally unfavour-able natural conditions in the South for agricul-ture, but at the same time acknowledges that farming is still far and away the predominant activity of the southern Italians for want of alternative means of livelihood. The result is that human beings suffer from the unpropitious nature of the physical conditions and endure depressing poverty with resignation to a harsh environment and to a substandard way of life.

Historical factors

The history of the Italian peninsula may be traced back to the time of Neolithic peoples from North Africa, who spread into a landscape of forest and marsh. They were succeeded by other peoples coming in from both the north and the south, but our knowledge of all these very early inhabitants is slender. However, by 500 B.C. more detailed knowledge is available. At that period there were a number of distinct cultural groups occupying well-defined areas within the peninsula. The Etruscans had spread well to the north from their territory between the Tiber and Arno; Venetians occupied the eastern end of the northern plain, and numerous small groups occupied the central Apennines and Adriatic littoral. Phoenicians and their colonists from Carthage occupied Sardinia and western Sicily and the Greeks held much of Sicily and the 'toe' and 'instep' of southern Italy. Thus at that time southern Italy's outlook and lines of communica-tions were with North Africa and Greece and not with northern Italy.

The Etruscans, who at their greatest held most of the land from northern Campania to north of the Po and founded such cities as Verona, Parma, and Bologna, were responsible for much deforestation. Land was cleared for agriculture and timber was also needed for construction, for shipbuilding, and for charcoal for the ore-smelting which provided the basis of Etruscan commerce. By 400 B.C., the Gauls moving into the Po valley were overcoming the Etruscans, while from lands around the Tiber mouth which until then possessed only local importance, Rome began a period of expansion which within two centuries gave her control of most of what is now modern Italy.

The Levantine traders, the Phoenicians, ap-preciating the value of harbours and ports of call at this narrow waist of the Mediterranean where the eastern and western basins are separated, from early times held Malta, parts of Sicily, and Sardinia in addition to their Carthaginian settle-ments across the Strait in Tunisia. Their Greek

The ruins of the temple of Neptune, Paestum. This Greek city, to the south of modern Salerno, was founded as early as 600 B.C.

rivals were more assiduous settlers and from the eighth century B.C. gradually founded a series of city-colonies in Sicily and, by 400 B.C., in southern Italy as far north as Gargano and northern Campania. This was Magna Graecia and included such famous cities as Croton, Sybaris, Metapontum, Poseidonia, Neapolis, Syracuse, and Agrigentum. Today a few columns and ruins of temples are all that remain as physical reminders of the Hellenic period in the South's history. Yet there are other kinds of reminders: the rich agriculture provided the basis for exports of wine, olive oil, grain, and wool and for this the Greek colonist extended the farmed area by systematically cutting down woodland. Further, timber itself became an important item of trade and the forested hills of Lucania, especially, were despoiled. We may trace the beginning of the deterioration of the land of southern Italy to these centuries, for in these hilly lands the tree roots and brushwood bind together and stabilize the soil and limit erosion; once they are removed the heavy winter downpours sweep away the topsoil and gulley the parent rock. Flooding, the silting of river mouths, and the creation of marshes that became malarial have been the result.

Rome grew at the expense of her neighbours. She ousted the Greeks after the Pyrrhic War (280–275 B.C.) and then went on to struggle with the Carthaginians and to defeat them in the Punic wars from which Sicily, Sardinia, and Corsica all fell to Rome. This succession of wars cost Rome dear in lives as well as money. There were fewer settlers available to colonize the new conquests and much of the land in the islands and the southern mainland was acquired in large holdings by wealthy Romans who farmed them with slave labour. Slave labour was more suited to the simple types of farming such as grain-growing and animal-herding, thus a reduction in the area under olives, vines, and fruits followed and when cheap grain became available from North Africa the area under grain in southern Italy and Sicily became reduced. The farming pattern came to emphasize more and more the herding of sheep, cattle, and goats and the large estates became ranches run by slave herdsmen. The less and less productive countryside supported a smaller population and large areas of Sicily, Calabria, Lucania, and Apulia became seriously depopulated. The wealthy Roman landowners showed little interest in their lands but lived in Rome off their estate revenues. The animals took an increasing toll of the brushwood and trees. Under the Empire the situation worsened, for the import of cheap food led to economic pressures which reduced the class of free proprietors and labourers until landless freemen and subsequently freed slaves were allowed to squat on large estates in return for rendering their labour to the patrician landowner. Thus a system akin to serfdom became established and was to persist for centuries.

The disintegration of the Roman Empire after A.D. 400 saw a series of invasions both from the north and, for southern Italy, from the sea. The Vandals seized Sicily and later parts of the southern mainland and sacked Rome itself, but in the sixth century they too fell to another naval power, the Byzantines. In the ninth century Saracen hosts brought Islam from North Africa in their conquest of Sicily and Sardinia and, like the Byzantines before them, breathed some new life into the southern economy and restored something of the old reputation of the South for the export of wine, olives, grain, and timber. Mirroring what was also occurring on a greater scale in the North, rich trading cities such as Naples, Salerno, and Amalfi also emerged. The period following the collapse of the Roman Empire thus saw a succession of invaders who raided, pillaged, and sometimes settled but did not drastically change the ordering of rural life. Local self-help and local loyalties became part of the pattern for survival and all over Italy in the growing towns and cities local self-government under dukes, local nobility, or magistrates gradually evolved after the eighth and ninth centuries.

The movement of the Christian states against the Moslems, who by the tenth century controlled almost the whole of the western basin of the Mediterranean, saw in the eleventh century the successful conquest by the Normans of southern Italy and then Saracen Sicily. They arrived as mercenaries in A.D. 1017 to support a revolt against the Byzantines, but subsequently began permanent settlement and conquest which they completed by the end of the century. The Normans with northern vigour created a United Kingdom of Southern Italy and Sicily in which their feudal traditions easily blended with the pattern of large serf-run estates. Thus a division of the peninsula, which in economic and social aspects is perpetuated to this day, was established early in the twelfth century. The South, where feudal nobility and town dignitaries were firmly under the control of the monarchy, became clearly separated from the mass of states and dukedoms in the Centre and North which comprised part of the Holy Roman Empire. Throughout the succeeding centuries, whether separate kingdoms of Naples and Sicily or combined in the Kingdom of the Two Sicilies under the Bourbons, the South remained feudal and rural. The Crusades severed the commercial ties with the Near East that had advanced Naples, Amalfi and other trading ports, and the balance of commercial development moved powerfully towards the North with the rise of numerous centres including Venice, Florence, and Genoa.

The invasions and dangers of invasion, the general lawlessness and feuding, the outright wars resulted in most of the rural population in the South concentrating in villages and towns tightly knit around the lord's castle or fortress, and usually on hilltops for defence against both human enemies and the malarial fevers of the lowlands. By the end of the eighteenth century agriculture in the South was stagnant and the blight of the *latifundi* was all too clearly evident. While progressive measures swept along a whole train of improvements in northern agriculture, in the South feudal serfdom persisted with the agricultural economy characterized by sheep- and goat-rearing, with transhumance, and a continuing reduction of forest and soil-cover. The returns from the scanty yields of wheat, wool, and olives were taken from the land to keep the absentee landlords and landowners in style at the court at Naples. The Bourbon administration was corrupt and inefficient, and investment in public utilities and in communications was neglected so that these and other infrastructure bases, necessary for economic advance, were missing.

Thus the people of the South and their conditions at the time of the Unification of Italy in 1861 must be judged in the light of the events of previous centuries. Successive periods of varied but mainly harsh foreign rule, the persistent poverty of a peasantry living under serflike conditions, the suppression of all liberal movements and brutal persecution by the reactionary and unenlightened Bourbon regime created a bitterness and resistance to all government by the southerner. The depredations of centuries had created the eroded, gullied landscape so common a feature over much of the hilly land of southern Italy; the mosquito-infested marshy seaboard tracts where rivers had for centuries been depositing the top soil from their drainage basins; a natural environment that man had been plundering for centuries and that could offer only a sparse return to the rudimentary, outmoded agricultural methods that still prevailed when the Bourbons were overthrown by Garibaldi in 1861.

Economic and social factors

It is clear that at the time of Unification the South was considerably poorer than the North. Its agriculture, carried out under harsher physical conditions than that of the North was more primitive in character and far less productive. It is estimated that the southern agricultural worker at this time produced 20 per cent less than his northern counterpart. The structure of southern agriculture typified by the large landowner and the small peasant, which sanctified a feudal or semi-feudal relationship between the two, was inimical to efficiency and to investment. The large landowners who had the means had no interest in sinking money into their estates, and the peasants who had the interest to improve their holdings lacked the means. Growing pressure of population pushed cultivation up hill slopes at the expense of the woodland (for climate in southern Italy allows cereals and vines to grow as high as 1200 m) which continued to be depleted for timber and for charcoal and by the ubiquitous goat. In 1820 Sardinia had one-fifth of its area in woodland, but by 1900 barely one-twentieth. The problems of erosion worsened and malarial marshes increased in area.

Industrial development was even more restricted than agricultural development in comparison with the North. From 1850 the North, especially Piedmont, had encouraged industrial developments and innovations and was aided by the new trans-Alpine roads and railways which brought her into close contact with the industrially advanced countries of Western Europe. The removal of protective tariffs caused many inefficient firms to go out of business; many were small and under-capitalized. It was the large firms, many supported by foreign capital, which now emerged and laid the basis of modern Italian industry in engineering, shipbuilding, and textiles. Southern industry was much more limited in scope and structure. Much of it was of artisan character whose inefficient and relatively high cost of production was only possible under the shelter of a high tariff wall and a paucity of communications that gave almost a monopoly in local markets.

The merging of southern Italy into the new United Kingdom of Italy (1860–1) in many respects worsened conditions in the South although great efforts were made during the remaining years of the century to rehabilitate the South's economy and to supply the infrastructure, responsibility for which had been shrugged off by the Bourbon government. Public works in the South had been much neglected as a result of a policy of keeping taxation at a very low level. This benefited the ruling classes, especially the large landowners and the merchant class, but was to the detriment of the mass of the population and to the kingdom's economic progress. Communications had advanced but little from the medieval period. At the time of Unification there were only 99 kilometres of railway (1798 kilometres for the whole country) and the roads were also limited in mileage, of poor surface and formed only a very rudimentary network. Thus poverty of communications in the South meant the retention of primitive ways of life and perpetuated subsistence-type farming or, at least, fostered local rather than national markets. It elevated disproportionately local administration and administrators and retarded economic advancement. Educational facilities were negligible and 90 per cent of the South's people over six years of age were illiterate, against 67 per cent in the North. Quality of life was low in the South and was substantially below that of the North at the time of Unification.

At the time of Unification when every reform seemed desirable a single legislation for the whole of Italy was instituted, regardless of the differing social and economic conditions in the rich North and the poor Kingdom of the Two Sicilies. Further, measures to abolish all feudal forms of land tenure were passed, but in many cases thanks to legal loopholes they were evaded and the Church, particularly, continued to buy up large estates when possible. An inquiry in Sicily in 1885 established that immediately after Unification some 200 000 hectares had changed hands under these enactments. This might suggest a break-up of the great feudal estates but, in fact, 52 per cent of the land went to enlarge already extensive properties, 41 per cent enlarged medium-sized properties and only 7 per cent went to new peasant proprietors.

After Unification a large programme was put in hand by the new State to bring the communications network of the South up to the standards of the North. By 1885 after twenty years of effort the South had one-third of the nation's railway mileage and by 1900 equalled the North in length of track per unit of area. However, the opening of the Suez Canal (1869), the Mont Cenis tunnel through the Alps (1871), and the integration of the former State systems into a comprehensive network gave substantial advantages to the industrializing North. The road system of the South was also expanded and improved and much capital was spent on aqueduct and water-supply improvement schemes. The early years following Unification saw real advances in southern agriculture and the acquisition of continental markets for its fruit and wine.

The establishment of a national market following political Unification led to the loss of the high tariff protection formerly enjoyed by the South against competition from the North, and also to the reduction of tariffs on imports from foreign countries. These measures, coupled with the continuing improvement in communications, opened the South to the industrial products of northern Italy and the last two decades of the nineteenth century saw a heavy decline in industrial employment in the South during a period of substantial pcpulation increase. This period also saw a halt to agricultural improvements in the South following the imposition in 1887 of a protective duty on imported grain. The import of cheap American grain had lowered prices and was unpopular with the large southern landlords. They were the chief beneficiaries of the higher prices following protection, for the peasant farmers grew grain for subsistence and not for sale. The higher prices led to the extension of the area under grain at the further expense of pasture and woodland, and strengthened the *latifundi* system of extensive, under-capitalized farming. These measures also resulted in counter-measures by France against Italian wine. These particularly hit the southern wines, then finding openings in the French market owing to the phylloxera scourge. Italy's loss was Algeria's gain.

It is now thought that until 1900 the gap between economic conditions in North and South widened only slowly, but this century it has widened much more rapidly. This reflects a multiplier element in the rate of advance in the secondary and tertiary sectors of the North's economy compared with the very slow changes in the traditional agriculture of the South. The closing decades of the nineteenth century saw conditions created in the North that were conducive to a rapid expansion of both industry and agriculture. The widespread adoption of hydroelectric power from the northern mountains lowered energy costs (they were about 40 per cent less than in the South) and infrastructure developments of communications and utilities gave a firm base for an expansion of industry that gained pace after the 1887 protective measures. Northern agriculture too was more modern in structure and system, was capitalized and advanced, whereas that of the South had changed very little from the time of Unification.

It will be seen that immediately after Unification the new State recognized the imbalance between North and South and regarded it as a duty to put into force policies that aimed at the modernization of the South and the evening-up of economic opportunity and advancement over all parts of the kingdom. Heavy investment was made in the South until the turn of the century, particularly in improving communications and water supplies. Early this century policies for the Mezzogiorno showed some change. These changes indicated more positive policies but, in fact, accomplished little. They included the provision of adequate domestic and agricultural water supplies, the easing of taxation on the peasant farmer and provision of credit facilities, and the offering of fiscal concessions to industry locating in designated industrial zones at Naples. These measures made no great impact: the funds allocated for the small farmers' credit scheme were too small and the real problems related to the maldistribution of land-ownership and the urgent need for comprehensive land-improvement programmes were avoided.

Thus measures had been put into effect to aid the South and for their time they were quite substantial. That they had little success is due to lack of integrated planning (separate *ad hoc* measures were too often the rule), to the resources allocated being too small for the task, and to overmuch emphasis on agriculture within the existing structural framework and too little emphasis on industry. Little industry, other than a few firms at Naples, was attracted to the Mezzogiorno. To the economic disabilities of remoteness from main markets and higher fuel costs, human factors were added. Northern industrialists looked askance at the illiterate, unskilled, country-cousin type of labour that the South offered; at the dearth of entrepreneurial ability; at the unprincipled commercial habits of the southerners; at the general unreliability of a people long used to inefficient and oppressive government and to a venal judicial system which permitted crime and corruption. Thus until the middle of this present century, a period when the North moved firmly into the industrial world, geographical, economic, and social environments in the South combined to resist the discrete and inadequate attempts to solve the southern problem; and the gap between levels of living in North and South widened considerably.

3 Instruments of Rehabilitation

The Cassa per il Mezzogiorno

Legislation affecting the Mezzogiorno, the allocation of substantial government funds and the establishment of new institutions to disburse them, assumed major proportions in the immediate post-war years. Between 1947 and 1957 no less than 340 laws affecting the South were passed by national and regional parliaments. Many more have been passed since then. Of all these measures the most important and far-seeing was the establishment in March 1950 of the 'Cassa per il Mezzogiorno', designed to be a chief instrument of government policy for the rehabilitation of the South. The conditions at the time shaped this instrument of policy and the character of its early measures. It had become widely recognized that previous attempts to grapple with the southern problem had failed mainly through lack of overall policy, lack of co-ordinated planning, and bad administration. The early post-war years saw the emergence of the relatively new subject of development economics, which required a detailed statistical knowledge of the field of operations and employed interrelated and co-ordinated schemes of government intervention as an important factor for change. The careful preparation of an overall integrated plan defining the targets and allocating investment for a number of years was the hallmark of this modern method of operation.

By 1950 the problems of the South were coming to be better understood, thanks to a growing body of statistics relating to its economy and society that was becoming available. Marshall Aid and the establishment of the International Bank for Reconstruction and Development (World Bank) which had begun to make development grants and loans, nourished the growing body of opinion favouring the new ideas propounded by development economists—a policy, a plan, massive investment in support, and a supra-ministerial body to carry it through. Those favouring major assistance to the South were reinforced by another sector of opinion that was coming to see the poverty-stricken South as a potential market for the reviving Italian industry which had lost substantial overseas markets owing to the war. SVIMEZ ('Association for Industrial Development of the Mezzogiorno'), founded at the end of 1946, was an important and influential body that supported this view, maintaining that the development of the South would stimulate employment and the general economy of the whole country.

Finally, and perhaps decisively, the mood of the South itself had to be reckoned with. Conditions had been worsening for years, land-hunger was acute, unemployment and underemployment had reached severe proportions. The apparent neglect of southern problems by the politicians at Rome infuriated southerners and inspired direct action. In this they were supported by the Communists, who were behind strikes and much of the invasion of, and squatting on, the large estates that occurred in 1949 in Sicily, Calabria, and Apulia. Thus there were also cogent political reasons for new and dramatic moves to solve the southern problem, and the creation of the Cassa was the outcome. The Cassa was not a replacement of the ordinary administration, which was to continue its normal investments in agriculture, public works, etc. The Cassa was to deal with the extra-ordinary works of considerable magnitude that it was realized would be necessary.

The Cassa was established as an executive body responsible to the Committee of Ministers for the South (this included the Ministries of Agriculture, Forestry, Industry and Commerce, Public Works, Labour and Social Welfare, Transport, and the Treasury). Initially the sum of 1000 thousand million lire (£600 million) was granted to the Cassa to carry out a ten-year plan of basic, mainly infrastructure development. The Cassa's work overlapped the fields of several ministries and one important attribute was the power of co-ordination of effort as a result of being a supra-ministerial authority. This power was more apparent than real and led to a number of difficulties in the early years. The Cassa operates over the seven regions already listed as comprising the Mezzogiorno and also over small parts of Latium (Frosinone and Latina provinces) and a few other small areas beyond the 'border'.

In addition to allotments from the government the Cassa was given authority to seek loans from abroad and to do all in its power to attract private investment, both Italian and foreign, into the Mezzogiorno. The World Bank has been an important source of such investment: its loans accounted for nearly 30 per cent of the Cassa's total investment during its first decade. Common Market sources of finance have also helped, notably the European Investment Bank, which during the 1960s made loans of over 300 thousand million lire (£200 million) to the Cassa. In its first seven years the Cassa's investments were non-industrial and at the beginning many of its measures, understandably, were of a 'first-aid' character. Emphasis was placed upon the rehabilitation of southern agriculture, the principal occupation in the Mezzogiorno, and also on modernizing and extending infrastructure. In the plan, drawn up by Italian and American experts, 77 per cent of investment was earmarked for agriculture, 11·5 per cent for aqueducts and drainage, 9 per cent for road building, and 2·5 per cent for tourism. Some modifications were made to these apportionments in 1952 and more funds were made available, but industrial development was not included. The work for agriculture covered land improvements (including drainage) and extension of irrigation; public works such as afforestation in hilly and mountainous parts; works connected with land reform and the furthering of agricultural mechanization. Coastal marshes, notably those of the Metapontino bordering the Gulf of Taranto and the Maremma north of the Mezzogiorno boundary, were drained and the malarial mosquito eradicated; and numerous small irrigation and power dams were created, especially in Calabria, Basilicata, and Sardinia. However, the Cassa's work in the early years has been criticized as representing 'assistance' rather than being directed objectively at promoting increased productivity, and certainly its efforts were dispersed throughout the South rather than being concentrated on those areas and in those fields where the greatest return could be attained.[1] The conditions of the time and need for 'first-aid' may account for these features but underlying were the growth policies of then-current economic thought, mainly associated with the names of Nurkse and Rosenstein-Rodan. These viewed growth as balanced development based on massive and widespread infrastructure investments.

During the period 1950–70 the Cassa's functions were continually being broadened as the wide ramifications of development planning became appreciated and better understood. In 1952 its life was extended to twelve years and

another £132 million was made available. A growing need to expand non-agricultural employment opportunities led to new policy formulation in 1957. From that year the Cassa actively furthered growth policies for industry (although it was 1959 before real implementation began) and it was granted more comprehensive powers as overseer of all forms of development in the South. It has helped to build hospitals and schools and has established labour training centres; it has aided farmers in making land improvements; within its first ten years it had installed main water supplies for over five million people. It has gone on to provide a source of water at all 'inhabited centres' and has helped local authorities to build systems for distributing this water to individual houses. It dealt with afforestation of mountain slopes and the creation of reservoirs, built 12 000 kilometres of aqueducts, and drained marshes. Twenty-nine thousand kilometres of new roads and improvements to old ones have made large areas of the South more accessible and generally have improved living conditions. It will be seen that the Cassa has proved a remarkably flexible instrument particularly responsive to the practicalities of the day-to-day situation, to the shiftings of higher policy, and to changes in economic development theory.

In 1961 the efforts at agricultural improvement by the Cassa, the land reform and irrigation agencies, and the Ministry of Agriculture were supplemented by the passing of the law establishing the Green Plan, and in 1966 the Second Green Plan was passed. These financed land, crop, and stock improvements and market development, and improved distributional facilities. They have begun the urgent task of consolidating fragmented holdings: the reform of holdings that were too small into larger, viable properties. The establishment of marketing cooperatives for packing, grading, processing, refrigeration, and transport of agricultural produce was furthered vigorously.

In 1965 the life of the Cassa was extended for a further period of fifteen years and more massive funds were allotted to it on an even greater scale than for the first fifteen years. Its funds between 1950 and 1965 totalled 2216 thousand million lire (nearly £1400 million), those allocated for the six-year period to 1970 totalled 2200 thousand million lire. More emphasis was to be placed on industrial development—in investment it took as much as agriculture and infrastructure together. The promulgation of a National Plan for all Italy led to readjustments of organization whereby southern planning was brought within

1. K. Allen and M. C. MacLennan, *Regional Problems and Policies in Italy and France,* p. 49. Allen & Unwin, London (1970).

the national planning framework. The Cassa's help to agriculture was restricted to the irrigated areas where the greatest return is to be expected and where alone agricultural population has been increasing. In these areas the small family farm, fostered by the land reform, will have continued life. Assistance by grants and loans for agricultural improvement outside these areas is the responsibility of the Ministry of Agriculture. More adjustments in the role of the Cassa took place after 1970 when it became more streamlined to deal with projects of special importance such as promoting new industrial zones, the expansion of metropolitan areas, and projects that concern more than one region. Its more localized activities were passed over to the new semi-autonomous regional authorities (see p. 42).

Thus broadly through the twenty-five-year period the Cassa has had the function not only of initiating development projects but of co-ordinating the main lines of development within every sector of the South's economy, investing the government monies allotted to it or obtained from other agencies such as the World Bank and the European Investment Bank, and attracting outside capital into development projects. Over the period 1950–70 almost £5000 million was invested in Italy's South: yet still the southern economy had not reached the stage of 'take-off' into self-sustaining growth, although growing agricultural productivity, changing occupational structures, and the beginnings of a substantial industrial sector suggest that if success has not yet been obtained, it is at least in sight.

Agrarian reform agencies

Piecemeal attempts at rural improvement in Italy in modern times began with the initiative of the occupying French in the early nineteenth century. During that century various attempts were made to reclaim marshland, master malaria, control erosion, improve river channels, and plant woodlands. In the twentieth century, between the wars, the Fascists made more attempts to drain, irrigate, and rehabilitate the countryside generally throughout Italy, the programme being termed *bonifica integrale*. To the modern visitor to the South it may appear that much rehabilitation of southern agriculture has its expression in land reform. This is not entirely so, but the works of the land reform agencies are often particularly impressive. This great movement also began in 1950 and although carried out by specially constituted organizations, operates under the aegis of the Cassa, which co-ordinates the work of the agencies and regards the reform activities as a major means of bringing about both agricultural and cultural advances in the South.

The immediate post-war years saw the culmination of agrarian discontent in the South in the form of strikes, riots, and seizure of land, which involved some loss of life. The broad causes of such a situation have already been outlined, the immediate causes relate particularly to the inter-war years, when emigration was discouraged but no southern problem was acknowledged by the government. Agricultural productivity fell behind the increase in population which in itself gave rise to pulverization and fragmentation of holdings into uneconomic sizes. With a high subsistence element among the farming population and no alternative forms of employment, the already wretched standards of living were worsened. There was acute land-hunger, most of the peasant holdings being rented, many on a share-cropping basis and most without security of tenure. In many cases small plots of land were rented only for the duration of one crop, the negotiations being in the hands of a succession of intermediaries. The *borghesia* class of medium and small landowners played an active part in these transactions, charging extortionate rents to peasants and often doing little farming themselves. Many had professional or local administrative activities to provide their principal source of income. They and the smaller group of owners of the *latifundi* have been particularly characteristic of the South. Most of the large landowners lived in Naples, Rome, or Palermo and showed little interest in their estates run by their agents, except to receive the revenues. Such conditions, irrespective of other factors, gave no incentive to improve the land and have for long been a main cause of the low productivity of southern agriculture.

The outbreaks of violence in the South, especially in Calabria, drove the Christian Democrats, then in power, to drop a general land reform bill for the whole country that was being discussed in parliament and to pass three 'extraordinary' laws during 1950. 'Legge Sila' (May 1950) laid down land reform rules for the Sila highlands and adjacent Ionian territories of Calabria; 'Legge Stralcio' (October 1950) covered other mainly *latifundi* areas of the mainland and Sardinia; and in December 1950 the 'Legge Siciliana' was passed by the regional government of Sicily.

Although differing in detail, the three laws set out to expropriate land from the large landowners, to determine what the landowner could retain, to pay recompense, and to redistribute the expropriated land to landless peasantry and holders of the smallest plots. It was recognized that area alone does not give sufficient ground for estimating the value and importance of an estate. One hundred hectares of orchards or vineyards would make a large estate in terms of revenue, whereas five hundred hectares of rocky grazing in the mountains could not be regarded as a large estate. Such factors were taken into account when deciding how much land should be taken; a landowner who farmed extensively lost relatively more land than one who had invested money in his farm, introduced irrigation, planted fruit trees, and so on. Particularly well organized and efficient farms which met terms laid down by the law were deemed 'model farms' and were exempted from expropriation. Most of these were in the North of Italy. Compensation for expropriation was paid in bonds at 5 per cent interest, payable in 25 years.

Enti di Riforma

EXPROPRIATION.

Land reform was carried out in three stages: expropriation, allocation, and transformation of the plots. By government decree special agencies were set up to administer land reform in the various parts of the country. These are known as 'Enti di Riforma' and the nine areas they administer are indicated on Fig. 2. In all, about 800 000 hectares were expropriated, barely 10 per cent of the total area over which the Enti had jurisdiction. The proportions taken by types of crop are shown in Table 3.

From this Table it may be deduced that most of the land taken was extensively cultivated and land in which virtually no capital had been invested and where there were no houses, no roads. The cost of transforming such land has been prodigious and the Italian land reform has

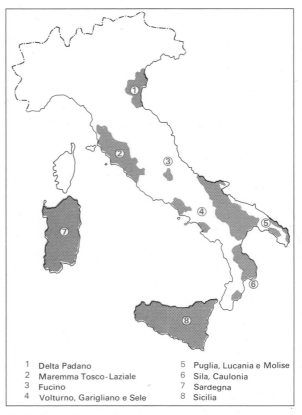

1 Delta Padano	5 Puglia, Lucania e Molise
2 Maremma Tosco-Laziale	6 Sila, Caulonia
3 Fucino	7 Sardegna
4 Volturno, Garigliano e Sele	8 Sicilia

Fig. 2. Land reform agencies and their regions

been one of the most expensive of such operations in the world.

Expropriated land had to be allotted to the peasants within three years and it was envisaged that the peasant farmer might participate in the works designed to improve his land. First priority

TABLE 3

Expropriated areas by types of crop

	per cent
Row crops	56
Uncultivated grassland and permanent pasture	28
Forests and productive uncultivated land	8
Sown areas with trees	5
Specialized tree culture	3
	100

Source: D. Scardaccione, *Agrarian Economy*, (Bari 1963).

in land allotment was given to share-tenants working under a land improvement contract and to landholding workers who were already permanently employed in the expropriated areas. Next in priority were wage earners and farm-hands having no property of their own and residing in the commune of the expropriated land. Then came workers living in neighbouring communes and finally smallholders, leaseholders etc. who were not self-sufficient. It will be seen that selection was based on need rather than ability. In all about 114 000 families received land, some 90 000 of them being in the Mezzogiorno. Whereas in the Maremma, Sardinia, and Fucino nearly all applicants were satisfied, in other parts of the South only 50–60 per cent of applicants were successful. Here the agrarian population was very dense and the land available inadequate. The fortunate recipients have to pay for their land by instalments over thirty years, the first two years being free of interest; after that a rate of 1 per cent per annum is levied. The price may not be paid off ahead of the thirty-year period and the owner may not sell or transfer any of the land until the full price is paid. These rules are designed to prevent the splitting up and fragmenting of the land, or even the amalgamation of properties that might recreate a *latifundi* system.

In allotting the land it was regarded as of first importance that viable family holdings (*poderi*) should be created. This meant a policy of settlement on the expropriated lands, with the building of farmhouses and the provision of the necessary public utilities and services. Except in the case of specialized crops the minimum size of farm needed to give an adequate standard of living in southern Italy is taken as 5 hectares (12·5 acres). For the country as a whole farms smaller than this minimum amounted to nearly 80 per cent

of the total number of farms and two-thirds of the farms had an area of less than 3 hectares. A high proportion of these miniscule holdings—worsened by excessive fragmentation—were to be found in the South. The size of farms allotted by the Enti depended upon the character of the land: in irrigated areas 4 to 5 hectares, but on hillsides in the mountains it could be 10 to 50 hectares. Where insufficient land was available to meet the demand or in the case of peasants owning some land, *quote* were awarded. These were small plots, insufficient in themselves to make a viable unit but adequate when used to supplement the income from land already owned or from other non-farming activities. Some 48 000 *poderi* and 65 000 *quote* have been awarded.

From the beginning, the reform was not regarded merely as a movement to redistribute land, but to bring about a lasting transformation in southern agriculture; it was to be agrarian reform rather than just land reform. Its mission was to bring changes to the South: in the structure of land-ownership, in the settlement pattern, in the types of farming, in the marketing of produce. It also sought to bring psychological change—to remove feudal mentality, to inculcate new ideas and make the peasantry receptive to change and new styles of living. Meeting these aims necessitated the provision of a considerable infrastructure involving provision of roads, domestic water supplies, electricity, schools, hospitals, and so on. On the agricultural side an extensive farming system had to be transformed into an intensive one and this involved detailed studies of soil character, water supplies, and proposed farm layouts, with recommendations for new crops or methods of husbandry. Further, the new farm units needed initial support: financial, agricultural, and social.

Land reform farms and farmhouses in the Metapontino. In the foreground on the right are bare stalks of tobacco plants, the leaves having been picked and hung on drying/curing racks placed in the sunshine round the house

A.B.M.

The fortunate new farmers were supplied with a house, appropriate sheds for livestock and implements, silos and compost pits. The siting of the houses is dependent upon the character of the land. In hilly country the development of a road network, provision of water supplies, and other necessities for scattered settlements would have been too expensive, so in such areas the new farmhouses are grouped together, in hamlet fashion, reasonably close to the holdings. On more level land a dispersed settlement pattern has been adopted, with the farmhouse built on the holding. In this, perhaps, has been the greatest social upheaval, for the majority of the new peasant farmers had lived in tightly-knit, often hilltop, communities in crowded dwellings on narrow streets and alleys where one's neighbour was almost part of the family. By placing the new farmer in a small detached house on his own land the former waste of time and energy in travelling often several miles to the scene of the day's work was avoided, and it became possible for the full energies of the farming family to be devoted to their new holding. However, an abrupt transplanting into so different an environment, at a distance from neighbours and perhaps some miles from schools, shops, and local administration was not carried out without some grumbling among the gregarious Italian peasants.

Service centres

The establishment of a number of 'service centres' was a partial response to these problems. The most complex type of such a centre becomes, in fact, a village. It has a nucleus of public buildings —town hall, church, post office, school, clinic, co-operative offices, social clubs, and cinema, plus shops and the houses of some of the agricultural families. More frequently the service centres are rather smaller and are built to serve the immediate needs of a peasant and farming population scattered over a radius of 5 to 7 kilometres from the centre. Such centres usually have church or chapel, school, clinic, recreational facilities, and a few shops. These centres act as both a social and business focus for the surrounding area and this has helped to tackle some of the needs of the families, many displaced from hill-towns. It is this new settlement pattern that provides a major element in the landscape transformation over many parts of the Mezzogiorno. Typical are the kilometres of new roads, so often paralleled with the open concrete conduits for irrigation water. Typical also is the orderly spacing along the roads of the new pink and white farmhouses with neatly tended plots of vines, tobacco, and vegetables that stretch from them. All this replaces former waste and malarial marsh or, at best extensive wheat- and olive-growing, and re-

Communal grain threshing organized by the local co-operative near Fucino in the central Apennines. In the background is part of the limestone flanks of the Gran Sasso d'Italia

A.B.M.

Green peppers being sorted and packed in a co-operative marketing centre in the Metapontino

presents a geographical change of the first magnitude.

The farmhouses in all the reform areas are built with an attractive simplicity of design aimed at keeping costs down and being entirely functional. These criteria mean that in each reform area a type-pattern prevails and that there are few variants from it. Only in more recent years have alternative designs become available. Except in upland areas most of the houses are of single storey design and can be extended without great cost. All are equipped with proper sanitary arrangements and with a modern cooker, usually fed by bottled gas. The first few thousand houses were built under contract systems and were designed as simple dwelling-units rather than a functional part of the agrarian transformation. The new owners were not enthusiastic and since the reform agencies dealt with faults and repairs the farmer found it difficult to regard it as *his* house. The impress of the individual was missing and to the southerner this was of some importance. Thus after the initial demands were met some agencies allowed new farmers to share in the

building of their own houses, overseeing plans and making financial contributions. In this way some variation of design has appeared, housing costs have actually decreased, and maintenance is done by the farmer himself, who now feels that the house is really his own.

From the beginning the land reform movement in Italy has fostered the co-operative. In some cases such an organization was necessary to take over the functions of the landlords in supplying machinery, fertilizers, etc. But it was stressed that proper co-operation reduces costs of production and permits the buying and loaning out of machinery which single farmers just could not afford. The co-operative is proving a useful instrument in the overall process of effecting change. Not only does it supply seed, fertilizer, and pesticides, operate agricultural machinery, organize marketing, but it serves as a centre from which demonstrations of new ideas, new crops, new methods of cultivation may be introduced to the small farmer. In addition to ordinary 'service' co-operatives a number of specialized co-operatives are also operated: these include

25

wine-making co-operatives, olive-oil mills, dairy co-operatives, and market garden co-operatives. All recipients of land grants are obliged to be members, for at least twenty years, of the co-operatives and associations that the Reform Agencies may establish. In this way full participation is possible and technical, financial, and economic assistance is available to guarantee and further the agrarian improvements that have been set in train.

Although the main considerations of the land reform were economic and technical, some attention has been paid to social ends; indeed, without some efforts here much of the agrarian advances and transformations might have failed. At least half the recipients of land have been casual labourers with little experience of acting on their own initiative. Most were accustomed to working irregularly and under orders on a large estate: the responsibility for making decisions rested on others. Adjustments to a new type of farming, to a new social pattern arising from new but dispersed housing among other assignees from different communes was not easy for those who were previously accustomed to living in a crowded hill-town. With limited means of transport most southern peasants rarely knew much beyond their own commune and whereas each family accepts its immediate neighbours, people from farther away—even from the next village—are regarded with reserve and even suspicion. Con-

sequently careful education and training for both social and technical ends was instituted from the beginning. Thousands of new farmers and their sons have attended courses on tree plantations and cultivations, on animal husbandry and farm management. For many, ideas of systematic land management were novel and the introduction of new tree crops, such as citrus fruits, necessitated special courses of instruction. Thousands of women have attended courses for rural housewives covering physical and domestic hygiene, elements of rural home economy, and explanations of the aims and place of land reform.

Fighting against illiteracy, agencies have organized courses for adults and, in association with the Ministry of Public Education, have established hundreds of new schools in the areas of the new smallholder settlements. There is no doubt that the last twenty years have seen considerable advances in both the quantity and quality of education in the South and that the land reform agencies have played an important part in this. All these measures contribute to the creating of a new social sense in the assignees. Most have moved up on the social scale and this involves the assumption of responsibilities, not merely for their own family farm, but for the running of the co-operatives. Thus for real success in the movement entrepreneurial ability, powers of leadership, and willingness to take the initiative are all qualities that are being sought and fostered.

4 Examples of Agrarian Reform

Land reform in Apulia

Space does not permit a study of the accomplishments of all the reform agencies, so three of the most important have been chosen to provide examples of their work and of the problems and difficulties with which they have had to contend. The area under the jurisdiction of the 'Ente di Riforma Apulia–Lucania–Molise' covers one and a half million hectares and is the largest of the reform areas. It stretches in a broad belt running south from the Gargano peninsula to the Metapontino along the coast of the Ionian Sea, with the addition of a small part of the Molise and small detached areas in the Salentine peninsula (the 'heel' of Italy). The areas not included are the mountainous regions of the Molise and Gargano, the western and southern areas of Potenza province, the Bari coastal strip and the Murgia dei Trulli to the south; both the latter are under intensive cultivation with an emphasis upon vines, olives, and almonds. Some 17 per cent of the area is classified as mountainous, 53 per cent as hilly and 30 per cent as plain. All the regions included were characterized by agglomerations of large estates, with poorly capitalized farming and a short-term relationship between owner, manager, and labour.

Apulia differs from the rest of the Mezzogiorno in having an abundance of relatively flat land; while Lucania (now Basilicata) is almost entirely mountainous. In the north the Tavoliere di Puglie is a vast plain of marine deposits occupying a former strait between the Gargano massif and the Apennines. The light clayey soils are parched and dusty in summer but heavy and sticky during the wet weather. Much of this area grows wheat, although in islands here and there the area under the vine increases. Part of this area was the scene of pre-war land settlement under the 'Opera Nazionale dei Combattenti' (the war veterans of the First World War) and for miles the plain is a chequerboard of small plots and O.N.C. farmhouses. To these have been added the Riforma additions since 1950. The southern edge of the Tavoliere is marked by the River Ofanto and south of this the more porous soils of underlying limestones are especially utilized for vines, olives, and almonds. The low limestone tableland of the Murge is extremely desiccated in the summer and seems almost devoid of population, which is to be found congregating into the few country towns that have grown up where water supplies are available. Here, against the Adriatic, climate is more extreme than on the western side of the peninsula and the summer drought is more prolonged. Hard wheat predominates on the lower areas of the limestone Murge but gives way to rough pasture, often with bare rocks protruding, at the high levels.

Apulian scenery owes much to the tree and bush crops which abound over so much of its lowlands and particularly over the Salentine peninsula: vines, olives, almonds, and fig trees, all frugal and drought-resistant plants. Except for sheep associated with rough grazing and being turned on to the wheat stubble of the *latifundi*, livestock have had only a limited place in the Apulian economy. Under the 'instep' of Italy, around the Gulf of Taranto and flanking the Ionian Sea, is the Metapontino. Across this narrow seaboard tract a number of small rivers, almost dry in summer, bring down the drainage and much of the topsoil from the Lucanian Apennines. They include the Bradano, Bassento, Agri, and Sinni rivers. Until after the Second World War much of this coastal plain was only accessible to the railway passing along the coast. It was dominated by very large estates, divided into large tenancies. The largest estate was that of Policoro covering 6000 hectares. There were scarcely any inter-farm or farm roads and the population was sparse. This was because much of the seaboard tract was marshy and the haunt of malarial mosquitoes. (See Fig. 4a, p. 30.)

Basilicata is a mass of bare, eroded mountains with steep raw slopes dropping to river valleys that for much of the year display choked courses and braided channels. Patches of cereals in hollows and mountainside pasture reflect the main lines of the poor agricultural economy. Yields everywhere are below the national average. Villages as well as towns perch on hilltop sites avoiding malarial lowlands. This unfavoured province has been exporting its able-bodied population in large numbers for over a hundred years.

The tasks facing this Ente were typical of those confronting all the agencies. It has had to cope with a variety of difficult environments; it has had to change a mainly extensive farming system traditional to those landscapes into an

Transformation in Apulia. The lines of gnarled old olives on a former estate being interplanted with young citrus trees, possible with the new supply of irrigation water (foreground)

intensive small-scale pattern; it has had to create a vast infrastructure of roads, houses, villages, water supplies, and services; and it has had former landless day-labourers (*braccianti*) as the major recipients of the new holdings, with many of them needing extra training. In the face of these problems very considerable progress has been made.

A total area of 200 867 hectares was expropriated from nearly 1500 landowners. This represented 12 per cent of the area of the land reform and a little over 5 per cent of the total area of the three regions. Most of the expropriated area was of the *latifundi* type with 96 per cent owned by absentee landlords. The expropriations were particularly heavy in the Metapontino and in the provinces of Matera and Foggia where, in the Metapontino and in the Tavoliere districts, there were heavy concentrations of large estates.

The Ente received 100 000 applications for land assignment; 39 per cent were from landless labourers, 26 per cent from tenants, smallholders, and share-croppers, and 35 per cent from tenants and owners who were not self-supporting. There were far more applications than there was land available and finally only 31 000 families were successful. In order to even out the ratio of land available to applications for assignment the Ente aided transfers of population, particularly from the mountains around Matera and Potenza to the Metapontino and from Gargano and the Apennines to the Tavoliere.

The change from an extensive farming system into an intensive one necessitated a substantial infrastructure of roads, water supply, power supply, etc. as well as reclamation of much land by draining, de-stoning, and so on; in all this work the Cassa gave financial assistance. The

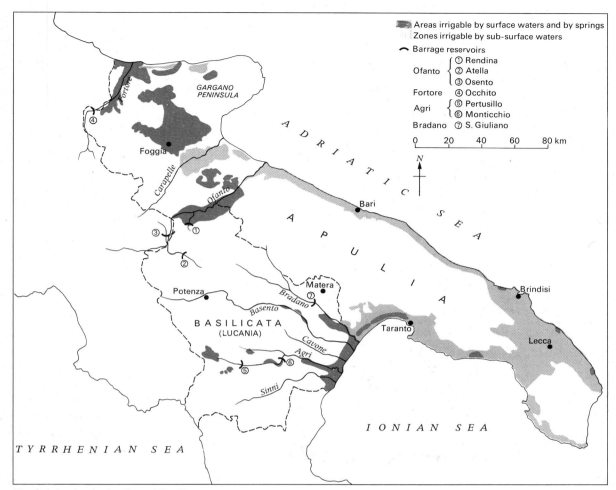

Fig. 3. Irrigation in Apulia and Basilicata

most far-reaching changes in the farming pattern become possible where irrigation water can be provided. Such a supplement to the low and seasonal rainfall permits assured returns and the growth of a wide range of crops, and effectively breaks the old 'wheat and olive' mentality. A vast programme of irrigation was undertaken by the Agency for the Development of Irrigation which has involved damming the upper valleys of the Bradano, Agri, Ofanto, and Fortore rivers to give a guaranteed supply of water to the Metapontino, the lower Ofanto and Fortore basins. Hundreds of wells have also been drilled to tap sub-surface water and springs in the Salentine peninsula and along the Adriatic coast (Fig. 3). This programme is vital to the transformation of agriculture, for it permits the growing of more remunerative crops such as citrus fruits. The plan to bring nearly 200 000 hectares under irrigation was well on the way to completion in the early 1970s.

Metapontino

With irrigation a tremendous transformation takes place, as is well demonstrated in the Metapontino, now a show-place for the efforts of this Ente. This former malarial coastal plain was reclaimed in the immediate post-war years, the malarial mosquito being wiped out with the (then) new D.D.T. and the marshy areas drained. Nearly 5000 families have been settled on the former waste or wheat-and-olive-land. The average size of farm is about 6 hectares. Land clearing, levelling and deep ploughing was carried out, roads built, farms laid out, farmhouses built, and irrigation conduits installed. In all, 8 million vines, 300 000 olive trees, 350 000 citrus and other fruit trees, and nearly three-quarters of a million pine trees for wind-breaks have been planted. Some 3000 farmhouses have been built. A new landscape has been created, clothed with high-income-yielding horticultural, industrial, and tree crops. Crops of oranges, mandarins, peaches, apricots, and pears can give ten times the return of the former, extensively-grown, wheat and olives. Salad crops, tomatoes, tobacco, sugar-beet, and the vine are the other principal crops of the new smallholders. A busy prosperity is now apparent. Mule carts are still to be seen but the roads hum with lorries and cars, small tractors and trailers, and the almost universal Vespa. The small houses are surprisingly well furnished, many boasting washing machine, refrigerator, and television set.

Some idea of the great task carried out by this land reform agency may be obtained from the bare figures of its accomplishments. In all it has built 15 000 farmhouses, 50 service centres, and 9 new villages. These are connected by nearly 1700 kilometres of new roads. About 7500 wells were bored and new planting includes 90 million vines, nearly 3 million olive trees, and almost 2 million citrus and fruit trees. The transformation of large areas of the landscape that these figures proclaim has brought positive benefits to many thousands and made distinct additions to regional productivity. Some population has been siphoned

from the mountains but the problems of the remaining hill-farmers and of the eroded mountain slopes have yet to be tackled in earnest. Further, the achievement of the Ente must be held in perspective: a population of over 1·5 million comes under its jurisdiction and about 65 per cent of the active population was concerned with agriculture. In this context the operations of the Ente and land allocation to only 30 000 families look less imposing.

Land reform in Calabria

In Calabria, Italy's rocky 'toe' the principal region subjected to land reform lies in the north and mainly comprises the Sila Plateau and adjacent areas. It comes under the jurisdiction of the Ente Sila and the provisions of the Legge Sila, which provides for the expropriation of plots that are liable for transformation and belong to owners with holdings in excess of 300 hectares.

In northern Calabria the Apennines change direction and composition, swinging due south and becoming crystalline instead of calcareous. They break up into semi-isolated mountain masses rising abruptly from the coast and are deeply scored by the ravines of the seasonal rivers and streams. The Sila Massif occupies nearly one-fifth of Calabria, stretching across its widest part

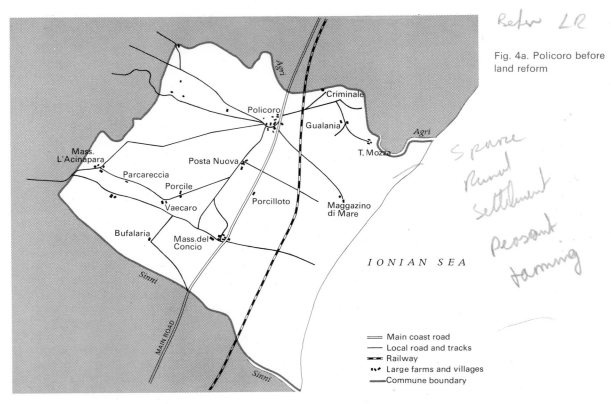

Fig. 4a. Policoro before land reform

Main coast road
Local road and tracks
Railway
Large farms and villages
Commune boundary

between the two seas. The highest part, Sila Grande, is composed of granitic rocks and attains over 1800 m. It is flanked by softer schists which have become harsh and steep from their dissection by the winter storms and snow-melt of spring, for snow rests on the upper parts of the Sila Grande for up to three months of the year. The heavier precipitation which these uplands engender (up to 1500 mm per annum) falls mainly upon impervious rock and the run-off is both voluminous and rapid. It is these seasonal torrents that have carved deep clefts in the schistose rocks and that do considerable damage to communications, riverside terraces, and the settlements nearer the coast.

The rolling plateau of the upper Sila offers a mixture of rough pasture, bog, and coniferous woodland. To reach it one passes from Mediterranean evergreen trees to magnificent forests of chestnut and beech reminiscent of more northerly parts of Europe. Until 1950 this extensive hilly area was one of the remoter parts of Italy and lay in the hands of a few large absentee landowners. It remained virtually undeveloped despite heavy pressure upon minutely-divided agricultural land in the surrounding lower-lying villages. Then practically no one lived in the Sila, the land was let and sub-let from the spring until the autumn

to pasture sheep and cattle from the lower areas. Crops of hay, potatoes, and rye were sown and gathered, and the pastures inadequately utilized.

About 10 per cent of the Sila (15 000 hectares) was expropriated and has been allotted to about 3500 families. The whole area has been ranked as one requiring reclamation and a tremendous amount has been done to improve its agricultural and pastoral potential and to open it to tourism. The special conditions of the Sila necessitated special selection of assignees and they have been restricted to those who have previously cultivated land on the Sila. The assignee has to guarantee that he will live all the year round on his new farm and not go back to the lowland village for the winter.

In the Sila Grande itself over 800 reform farmhouses have been built to settle the new permanent population. Generally they are grouped in hamlets of perhaps half a dozen dwellings, each being of substantial two-storey construction with barn and stable. A mixed farming economy is being fostered with some stress on animal husbandry—the new farmers are supplied with up to forty (mainly Brown Swiss) milk cattle per family—and on improved pastures (clover has been introduced), potatoes, and some deciduous fruits. In the highlands there are three artificial

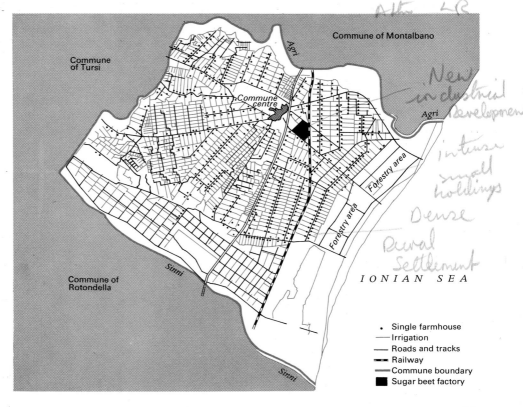

Fig. 4b. Policoro after land reform

31

The deeply dissected schist country on the western flank of the granitic Sila Grande. Note the choked river bed and cultivation on steep slopes

lakes, created for hydro-electric power production. Beside one of them, Lake Arvo, and amid magnificent scenery, the tourist resort of Lorica has been built. In the deeply eroded hill country surrounding the Sila Grande tremendous remedial work is being attempted, for here population pressure has led to the cultivation of steep slopes and has caused dreadful erosion and gulleying. Little of this land is subject to land reform laws and in any case it is inadequate for the population. Here emigration and movement to non-agricultural occupations seems the only answer to this problem of rural overcrowding.

The Ente Sila has faced different problems on the coastal lowlands to the east. North of Crotone up to the Sibari plains irrigation has been introduced and successful smallholdings now grow citrus, melons, tomatoes, tobacco, and cotton. However, south of Crotone the Marquesato area has been less amenable. Here, near the coast, sandstones rest on clays and inland are grey Pliocene clay hills devoid of vegetation and gulleyed into almost surrealist landscapes. The poor grey soils, sticky and unworkable in winter, parched and dusty in summer, still produce little but poor crops of wheat. Up to one-third of the

A hamlet of new land reform farmhouses in the open 'Alpine' scenery of the Sila Grande at nearly 1800 m

newly installed farmers could not make a living and gave up their holdings after two or three years. The holdings were too small, bearing in mind the low returns with this type of farming. The lack of irrigation water (in one of the driest parts of Italy) precluded attempts at intensive farming.

Land reform in Sicily

One-quarter of the population of the Mezzogiorno is to be found in the island of Sicily and, except locally in Calabria, here is to be found the greatest population pressure upon limited resources within the whole republic. Here also is to be found some of the greatest poverty. Sicily is an island of contrasts: between the watered coastal fringes and the baked, arid interior; between the traditional growing of pitiful crops of wheat and, where water is available, lush critrus groves; between extreme poverty of the masses and great riches of the few; between the Catania–Augusta–Siracusa industrial area and the backward agricultural remainder of the interior.

Topographically and geologically the island is a continuation of the mainland. The mountains overlooking the Straits of Messina are of gneiss and schist like their counterparts behind Reggio di Calabria. Farther inland are sandstone heights and then rolling country of sandstones, conglomerates, and clays; to the west are mainly plateau-like areas of limestones, including karstic features. The great heat of summer bakes the interior clay lands to a solid dusty surface; the low annual rainfall falling in winter storms sweeps away traces of soil from the long-denuded clay slopes; gulleying and landslips continue the destruction of centuries. The rolling hilly country in the interior of Sicily is little more than a desert.

In many respects Sicily is a world apart from the rest of Italy. Its long history, a succession of conquests and occupations—the Greeks, the Arabs, the Normans among the many—has bred a hard people with mutual dislike and distrust between them and the mainland. The separateness of Sicily was enhanced in 1946 by the immediate grant of its own regional government, whereas for much of the mainland this form of government was only conceded in 1970. To some extent these facts account for the marked differences in land reform operation and its comparative lack of success. The feudal mentality remains heavily on the island with the large landowners very much in control. Their estates are rented out to agents and intermediaries who let out the land in small plots to the peasants. The Legge Sicilia is more complicated than the other land reform laws and allows of so many loopholes and avenues of appeal that the whole process has taken far longer than on the mainland and for the most part success has been minimal. Large properties still exist and less than 100 000 hectares have been expropriated. An enormous administration has been built up under the Ente per la Riforma Agraria in Sicilia (E.R.A.S.), much of it by patronage, until a top-heavy bureaucracy has resulted. One-third of the E.R.A.S. budget in the decade 1950–60 went on administrative costs.[1]

Inefficiency and poor planning, in part due to the lack of enthusiasm of the officials, has seen the building of hundreds of two-roomed farmhouses of inferior design and construction and unsuitable for the great heat of the Sicilian summer. In many cases roads and services were not ready when the houses were completed and the allotment of three to six hectares of unimproved clay and rock was as inadequate as a one-bedroomed house to provide for the large peasant families. The result has been the desertion of the houses and holdings over many parts of central Sicily. There is in any case a marked aversion by most peasants to leave their crowded hilltop villages and towns to live in dispersed fashion kilometres away in the lowlands. Further, traditional cereal growing dies hard despite the fact that with poor yields it is a form of agriculture quite unsuited to the needs of the Sicilian family. The E.R.A.S. has made little progress in solving these all-important human problems of the reform programme. It has also made only slow progress at dam-building to supply water for local irrigation, yet it is upon the provision of water that improvement of Sicilian agriculture depends. Much of the land reform in Sicily has been a failure and in any case the rigid division of land into small holdings would seem to be wrong on the poorer clay lands; large mechanized farms might be more successful. This would be opposed to land reform policy, for it would worsen the unemployment problem, but with either approach, emigration would seem inevitable for much of the Sicilian youth.

An evaluation of the land reform

Although the work of the land reform agencies continues, virtually all their expropriations under the three laws have been completed and some assessment of their accomplishments over twenty years is now possible. Bearing in mind that a small area of the Po delta and the Maremma were

1. R. King, 'Mediterranean island in torment', *Geographical Magazine*, **44**, p. 182 (1971).

included, out of a total reform area of eight million hectares some 800 000 hectares were expropriated. About 113 000 families benefited in the redistribution of this land. These figures are significant, but small when taken in a national context.

A principal object of the reform was to change the usage of land, to create a greater intensity of land use, and to make more productive the undeveloped *latifundi*, at the same time introducing labour-intensive crops suitable for small family holdings. Where it proved possible to install irrigation facilities such changes have had considerable success. The figures published (to 1965) are shown in graph form (Fig. 5) and show a fall in cereal production and a rise of flowers, fruit, and industrial crops (sugar beet, tobacco, tomatoes, etc.). In livestock great changes have also taken place. Cattle numbers rose from 12 000 to 127 000 on reform land; pigs from 13 000 to 90 000; sheep from 42 000 to 203 000; and small animals (poultry, rabbits, etc.) from 218 000 to 1 786 000. These are material changes and in terms of gross saleable production on assigned land the output rose from 70 000 lire per hectare in 1951 to just over 200 000 lire in 1965. In a few well-run intensive but capitalized small farms in the Metapontino and Campania, gross saleable product probably reaches £1000 per annum (1·5 million lire). It will be realized that individual incomes of assignees differ considerably, dependent upon the type of land, size of holding, amount of labour available, degree of capital reinvested, and so on. Thus it is not possible to give meaningful average-income figures.

The social effects of the reform have been telling. Except probably in Sicily, the power of the large landowner has been broken or whittled down, although generally the *borghesia* class has been unaffected. After early years of over-paternalism the Enti di Riforma have had some success through the co-operatives in getting the new owner-farmers to identify themselves with the movement and to exert some initiative; but for many the co-operative merely replaces the old landowner in the provision of seeds, fertilizer, and instructions. The spread of settlement into former open country has made landscape changes of great magnitude. Some 45 000 farmhouses have been built in the various reform areas (most *quote* recipients did not receive a house and not all *poderi* assignees changed their residence) and most of these were in the form of dispersed settlement upon the assigned lands. These transfers—essential if such development was to succeed—were revolutionary for the South and may start a trend of movement out from the traditional hill-top towns and villages.

The Cassa has ably supported the Enti with the provision of infrastructure and service works, and private capital also has played a part, especially investing in industrial plant comple-

Fig. 5. Land-use changes in land reform areas, 1953–65

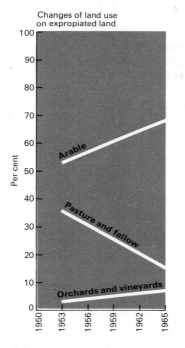

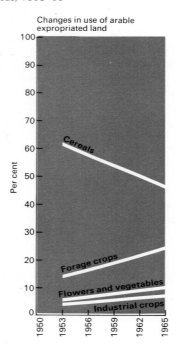

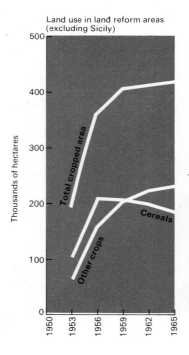

mentary to agriculture such as oil mills, a sugar mill, and fruit preserving plant. Nevertheless emigration from the South continues at a high rate and is thought by some to endanger southern development. It has been pointed out that there are more peasants from the South living abroad than there are living and working on Italian soil. However, it must be realized that as agriculture in the South is modernized, a movement of population from it is to be expected. Land reform which puts emphasis upon more intensive production affects only a small part of southern agriculture and even so, as the family holdings become more efficient and more mechanized, their demand for labour becomes reduced. Alternative employment in the South although increasing, is inadequate to provide for the large numbers involved and migration continues; some go to settle, but others to work for a period, in the North or in other Common Market countries. Remittances back from these workers are valuable additions to southern income, but some feel that they do not recompense for the youth and life that is being drained away from southern villages.

It is not easy to assess briefly the degree of success of the attempts at rural transformation. In some areas, for example in the Campania and the Metapontino, great advances have been made, but here geographical conditions were favourable and this is of importance in the harsh physical reality of the South. Less success has attended efforts in the poorer hilly land. One reason is probably that the Enti's land allocations were not generous enough and even at best in, for example, the Sila, incomes are well below those of the irrigated lowlands. Now a policy of agglomerating the inadequate smallholdings into more viable units is being pursued. The land reform may be criticized under several heads, the size of holdings being one. The social mood of the time laid stress on peasant-ownership but

this conflicts with the economic trend under the E.E.C. which is for larger operating units in order to enjoy economies of scale. This is a problem that may have to be resolved in the future, for what is now a viable unit may no longer be one a decade hence—especially since with economic development acceptable minimum standards of living are likely to rise. The economically independent yeoman has never existed as a class in Italy and Common Market development seems destined to make the attempt to create such a class short-lived.

A further criticism concerns its very limited scale: only 10 per cent of the total reform area was actually expropriated and the fact that only a handful of peasants benefited made them into almost a privileged class. The high cost of the reform has also excited much comment. Official figures of costs are put at £470 000 000. The costs of land reform per hectare may be as high as £600, and the cost of settling each family averages £5300. These remarkably high figures reflect the large amount of poor and indifferent land taken over by the Enti.[2]

However, one must look beyond the present and beyond the spread of little farms to the less obtrusive works that are continuing: the stabilizing of slopes, the heavy programmes of afforestation, the general checking of soil erosion and gulleying, the confining of river channels. Much more of this work is needed and will be undertaken as hill-farms are gradually eliminated and the upland areas rehabilitated. These are important long-term measures for the South that will give an increasing return with the years, as will the more apparent infrastructure of good roads, drainage, and services that were scarcely dreamt of twenty years ago.

2. R. King, 'Structural and geographical problems of South Italian agriculture', *Norsk Geografisk Tidsskrift*, **24**, p. 91 (1970).

TABLE 4

Division of the Cassa's annual expenditure by sectors, 1950–65 and 1966–9

| Sector | 1950–65 | | 1966–9 | |
	Value thousand million lire	Percentage by sector	Value thousand million lire	Percentage by sector
Industry	10·1	6·9	110·7	36·0
Agriculture	82·9	56·1	76·2	24·7
Tourism	6·2	4·2	24·8	8·1
General Infrastructure	33·1	22·4	60·3	19·6
Others*	15·3	10·4	35·8	11·6
Total	147·6	100·0	307·8	100·0

*Technical assistance, management training, etc.   *Source:* K. Allen and M. C. MacLennan, op. cit. p. 77.

5 Industry and Tourism

(10 POINTS) PROBS OF EST. ING INDUSTRIES.

Industrial development in the South has lagged a long way behind that of the North. Attempts to find employment opportunities outside agriculture led to a considerable inflation of the tertiary or 'service' sector of the economy, mainly by large numbers of self-employed eking out a living from some kind of retail trade. An examination of the pattern and structure of industry during the early years of the Cassa's life reveals the typical dual division regarded as normal today in developing countries. This division is between traditional, often family establishments, small scale and thinly capitalized, and a few larger industrial plants, well organized and capitalized and using hired labour and modern methods of production. The first group tends to supply local markets with goods related to local resources (e.g. food, clothing, and products of the wood and furniture industries) and generally, with rather primitive production methods, unit costs may be relatively high. The modern industries aim at wider markets and produce the type of manufactured goods that suit demand at higher income levels (e.g. engineering and chemical products, textiles, paper, and rubber products).

In 1951 industrial employment accounted for only 11 per cent of the working population in the South and in manufacturing industry alone it was 8 per cent, whereas that of the North was 21 per cent. Further, the overall efficiency of southern industry was less than in the North; around 1961, value added per industrial employee was reckoned to be only about 60 per cent of the northern level. In that year 44 per cent of industrial employees in the South were in establishments employing not more than ten workers and 20 per cent of industrial employees in the South were in tiny establishments comprising a maximum of two employees.[1] In the North of Italy over 80 per cent of industrial employees were in concerns employing more than ten workers. Until the early post-war years the only real centre of industry in the South was Naples, the former capital of the Kingdom of the Two Sicilies. Industry here received a fillip in 1904 when a special law established industrial zones and permitted fiscal and

1. K. Allen and M. C. MacLennan, *Regional Problems and Policies in Italy and France*, p. 31. Allen & Unwin, London (1970).

customs concessions to attract industry into them. During the inter-war period a number of engineering and metal industry firms (several of I.R.I. origin) became established; textile manufacturing increased, as did shipbuilding and the construction of locomotives. Industrial development in other towns of the South was negligible.

The need to expand industry in the Mezzogiorno was well realized when the Cassa was instituted in 1950 but the disabilities to industry posed by the South's harsh endowment, its agricultural background and tradition, its remoteness from the bustling go-ahead parts of Italy, its unskilled population, its paucity of infrastructure, all deterred industrial development. The urgent need to provide alternative employment to agriculture, to ease that sector of the economy and to reduce unemployment and under-employment were appreciated, but deemed to be largely impracticable during the early years of the Cassa's existence. Thus the Cassa's early role was to breathe new life into southern agriculture and to improve environmental conditions by infrastructure provision and improvement. This non-industrial policy was carried out until 1957 and saw considerable spending on the modernization of communications, water supply, and drainage. It was hoped that the development of such infrastructure facilities and the increase in agricultural incomes derived from the infrastructure works would expand demand in the South and thus generally create a more attractive environment for the growth of industry. This optimism was misplaced; for many years infrastructure provision remained below that of the North and the slowly growing southern markets were of little interest to northern firms compared with the markets already present in the North and in the adjacent countries of Western Europe. The lack of industrially trained labour in the South and the lack of ancillary and service firms that major plants rely on for components, raw materials, and engineering servicing (external economies) remained strong deterrents.

By 1957 it was realized that more definite intervention by the Cassa to attract and aid industrial development was becoming essential. In that year the Industrial Areas Law was passed— a very important law for southern development. It authorized the Cassa to support the establish-

TABLE 5
Changing importance in Southern manufacturing industry, 1951–66

Industrial group	Percentages on values at current prices			
	1951	1956	1961	1966
Food, drink, and tobacco	37·12	34·86	29·60	27·99
Textiles	4·72	2·69	3·16	2·93
Clothes, shoes, and leather goods	13·61	9·96	10·05	9·50
Timber and furniture	8·66	9·92	9·23	7·03
Metallurgical	4·05	5·57	5·70	7·74
Engineering	12·77	14·32	15·18	17·00
Transport	2·26	3·18	3·35	2·80
Processing of non-metallic minerals	6·97	9·46	11·50	9·36
Chemicals and petroleum- and coal-derived products	6·52	6·56	7·96	11·14

Source: G. Miconi, 'Southern Italy—some considerations', *Review of Economic Conditions in Italy*, **22**, p. 279 (1968).

ment of industrial zones in especially favoured areas and to aid in those areas the work of proposed consortia in infrastructure provision and improvement works aimed at attracting industry. The Cassa commissioned planning bodies to assist it in determining policies and discovering how they might best be applied, and from 1959 measures were introduced progressively to further southern industrialization.

In 1965 when the Cassa's life was prolonged (until 1980) a third phase in its work for the South began. More money was made available and the aim of industrial development was given priority. A new factor that had to be taken into account was the requirement to co-ordinate work in the South with the new National Plan. This involved the Ministerial Committee for the South being absorbed into a new national planning body which lays down policies and plans for the Cassa to carry out. The change of emphasis in favour of industrialization is shown clearly in the divisions of expenditure for 1950–65 and in 1966–9 (Table 4). It will be seen that from a bare 7 per cent of total funds in the earlier period, industry took 36 per cent in the later one and the amount to be spent on industry in four years was almost eleven times the amount spent on it over the previous fifteen years. Further, agriculture suffered not only a relative decline but also an absolute one; its total funds were reduced.

Industrial strategy

The measures that have been taken since about 1960 to industrialize the Mezzogiorno fall into three related parts: inducement, stimulation, and concentration. The first heading covers a wide range of incentives that were devised to offset those disabilities of the South that deterred the arrival of new industry. Under the 1957 law local authorities in designated development zones were each encouraged to form a consortium to develop basic infrastructure works such as road and rail links, water and power supplies, to expropriate suitable land, to improve environmental conditions for industry, and to offer varying inducements (such as buildings for sale or rent) to attract industrialists. The Cassa besides providing part of the capital for the work of the consortia was also allowed to make capital subsidies to help modernize medium and small industries in all but the largest urban centres. These grants and the loans that were also available, could make up as much as 85 per cent of the total capital invested. The amount made available was greater if the proposed location was within the designated growth areas, and in this case grants could also be awarded to large firms. There was also fiscal inducement such as a ten-year exemption from tax on industry and exemption from customs duties on imported equipment and, at the discretion of local authorities, part or total exemption from local taxes. Credit institutions backed by the Cassa made loans available to new industries and there were also small rail-freight concessions. It will be seen that this range of concessions was based on capital and favoured capital-intensive industry, and that they were not particularly favourable for the larger private firms.

The measures for stimulating new industry to move to the South hinged upon the government-controlled firms operated by the I.R.I. These firms had not shown much interest in the South

A.B.M.

New factories for sale or letting by the Consortium for the Industrialization Nucleus of Vasto, a small Adriatic coastal town

before 1957, but after that year an earlier law was enforced that instructed these firms to invest at least 60 per cent of any new industrial investment in the South. By 1964 40 per cent of their total investment was required to be in the South. Thus during the decade 1960–70 enormous capital investment in the South was made by the large state-controlled firms such as Italsider (iron and steel), E.N.I. (oil and gas), and Breda (mechanical engineering). As a result of the nature of most of the I.R.I. firms, emphasis was on basic heavy industry, but without the establishment of such industry in the South the prospects of attracting lighter consumer goods types of industry were deemed to be poor. An enormous investment of around 2500 thousand million lire (£1500 million) had been made by 1970, mainly in the fields of iron and steel, engineering and shipbuilding, petrochemicals, and cement manufacture. The establishment of substantial off-shoots of government-controlled firms in the South was expected to stimulate private organizations also to set up

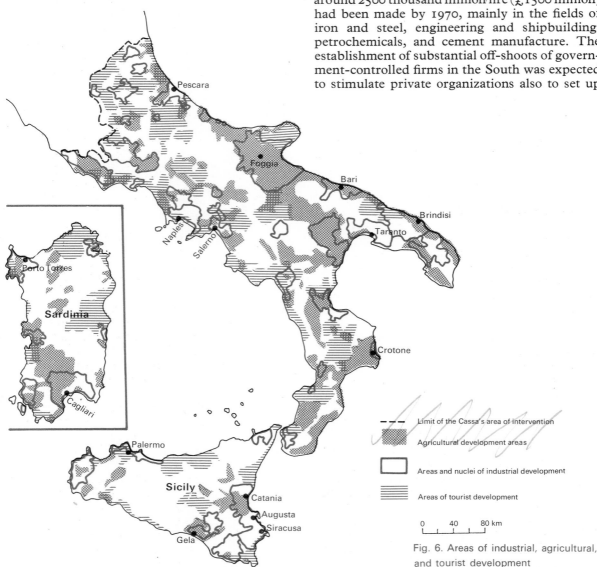

- – – Limit of the Cassa's area of intervention

Agricultural development areas

Areas and nuclei of industrial development

Areas of tourist development

0   40   80 km

Fig. 6. Areas of industrial, agricultural, and tourist development

southern branches, but the response was disappointing. Many of the new 'forced investment' plants have not paid their way and require continuing government or regional support. For the quinquennium 1971–5 the government greatly increased its allocation of money to the Cassa to help further industrial development and raised the obligation of the government controlled firms to place 80 per cent of their new industrial investment in the South with 60 per cent of their total investment to be there.

The concentration of new industry in the South into selected 'growth areas' was in response to changing theories in development studies and to the realization that a major deterrent to large firms locating in the South was the lack of external economies (the general advantages of an industrial environment). If industry coming to the South were established in a limited number of centres, then it was hoped that external economies would emerge there and at least in those areas an industrial milieu like that of the North might be created. By concentrating development measures into areas selected as being capable of rapid growth a much faster rate of growth and at lower cost was deemed to be possible. The region as a whole would benefit from the spin-off of development benefits from the growth centres. With such concentration, infrastructure provision is much cheaper, the costs being shared by numerous consumers closely located and, with varied industries, a pool of diversified and trained labour would become available.

Decisions as to the location of the designated industrial zones were not imposed by Rome but left to the initiative of local administrative and commercial bodies. If they desired such development they had to produce plans conforming to specific rules and requirements and submit them for approval. The role of the central authorities has generally been to adjust or modify many of the proposals. A total of forty-two of these growth zones had been approved or were about to be approved by 1970 (Fig. 6). Twelve of these were of some size and were designated Areas of Industrial Development, the remainder were smaller and were called Nuclei of Industrialization. The general desiderata for these zones to be delineated were some industry already in being, adequate power supplies, good communications, water supplies and a positive attitude to industrialization. As the map shows, the 'Areas' and 'Nuclei' are scattered over southern Italy and this raises the question of whether they are not too numerous and too scattered to fulfil the original idea of concentration into a few growth zones or 'poles'.

Only time can answer this, but it should be noted that the Nuclei are small (total population not more than 75 000) and are expected to attract smaller firms interested principally in the local markets; it is the Areas (population of not less than 200 000) that are designed as the main instruments of the industrial-complex policy. In this respect direct comparisons are possible with Spanish regional development policy. In fact, the Spanish Government enlisted the aid of Italian planners in determining which should be the Andalucian 'poles of growth' in the 1964–7 and 1968–71 development plans.

Industrial development

Since the mid nineteen sixties considerable infrastructure and industrial development has been accomplished in these Areas and Nuclei. A new impetus has come to life in such places as Naples and Salerno, Catania and Siracusa in eastern Sicily, Latina just south of Rome, Pescara on the Adriatic, and the triangle embracing Bari–Brindisi–Taranto. As far back as 1959 the latter three towns had been selected as a particularly favoured group under the new industrial-complex policies and they were designated 'industrial development zones'. By discriminatory investment and careful selection of industries to be established it was felt that 'poles of expansion' could be created, capable of transforming the local Apulian economy into one of dynamic growth. Following this, the European Economic Community designated this triangular part of Apulia as a 'pole of regional development' and in 1962 set in motion careful studies of the area's economy as a preliminary to drawing up a detailed plan for its development. Italy's Mezzogiorno is the Common Market countries' most under-developed area, and the interest of the Community led to one of the first major actions taken by the E.E.C. to implement that part of the Treaty of Rome which calls for reduction in the inequality in the economic development of different regions within the community. A comprehensive input–output table of the region was compiled to show the goods and services consumed and produced in all the current productive activities. From an analysis of this table new industries that would find the region's resources advantageous were determined and feasibility studies made for each of them. A list of over 200 'possibles' was reduced to 30 and from the proposals, made public in 1965, a concentration on mechanical industries was proposed for Bari and Taranto and on petrochemical industries for Brindisi.

39

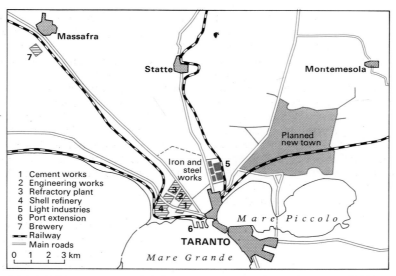

Fig. 7. Industry in the vicinity of Taranto

Bari–Brindisi–Taranto

Meanwhile momentum had already been gained in the area thanks to the Cassa's infrastructure improvements and to the 'forced' investment from a number of State-controlled firms. Port improvements, a small oil refinery, and plant producing a variety of engineering products (especially pipeline valves and control systems) were already installed at Bari. At Taranto from 1960 the great iron and steel plant was constructed by Italsider. An initial investment of £200 million established the plant on eight square kilometres of former olive groves at the edge of the town and only just over a kilometre from the sea. New jetties, wharves, and overhead transporters were installed to deal with bulk iron ore imports from Venezuela, North Africa, Liberia and coal from the U.S.A. and to export finished steel. Limestone is the only raw material found locally, but the coastal situation is exploited to the full. Sceptics have been confounded: the plant has proved a great success (one of its specialisms being steel pipes for oil and gas pipelines) and a series of enlargements have followed. It is now Italy's largest single iron and steel plant and has an annual capacity of 10 million tonnes. Over 5000 were employed when the plant first opened, out of the 50 000 who applied for jobs. Other industrial developments included a large cement works, an oil refinery, engineering works, and an estate of light industries (Fig. 7).

The E.E.C. plan involved the investment of £100 million and hoped to further nine main industries, producing pumps, agricultural machinery, mechanical excavators, cranes, machine tools, and various domestic appliances. They in turn would require 30 auxiliary industries concerned with repairs, tooling, foundry work, pressing, moulding, and galvanizing. It was hoped that such an agglomeration of varied basic and service industries would in turn attract other industrial investment, especially of medium-sized private firms but this has not yet occurred and the plan *per se* may have failed. At Brindisi the great chemical firm of Montedison has an extensive petrochemical plant producing ethylene and a range of raw materials for the plastics industry.

Naples

A teeming city of 1 300 000 inhabitants, Naples has now dropped in position to Italy's fifth port (after Genoa, the oil port of Augusta, Trieste, and Venice) and despite improvement works being carried out its future lies with industrial development rather than with its port facilities, although shipbuilding and ship repair work continues. State-controlled industry dominates the area with the Bagnoli iron and steel plant, the Cotoniere Meridionali cotton textile plant and the new Alfa Romeo car plant, opened in 1972. Among private firms Olivetti make office equipment and calculating machines at Pozzuoli; there is an oil refinery and the Montedison group has a number of plants producing plastics, chemicals, electrical equipment, and building components. The decision to establish a major car assembly plant near Naples was taken in 1967 after bitter argument. The establishment of Alfa-Sud, a subsidiary of Alfa Romeo, a small quality-car firm, by aiming to produce 300 000 cars a year brings that company into direct competition with Fiat who wanted the car industry to remain in the North. It was hoped that the establishment of this great assembly plant near Naples would induce numerous other subsidiary supplying firms to establish nearby. Whereas 15 000 new jobs were provided by the car factory, a total of 50 000 new jobs was envisaged if supporting firms also located in the area; unfortunately the middle years of the 1970s saw economic recession and reluctance of private industry to make new investment and take on such new ventures. Meanwhile Fiat has linked with the I.R.I. in establishing an Aeritalia aircraft firm near Naples to form the heart of a national aircraft industry.

Sicily

In Sicily the three designated industrial Areas are Palermo, Catania and Siracusa and these are supplemented by five Nuclei. The E.N.I., the State oil and gas group, has established a £150 million petrochemical plant at Gela on Sicily's south coast. The small output of thick and sulphurous oil at local wells is augmented by Middle East crude oil brought in by tankers to the new jetties. The plant produces fertilizers, polythene and synthetic fibres. The recent establishment of a car assembly plant near Palermo by Fiat (to produce 50 000 small cars a year) marks one of the recent moves of this private firm into southern investment. The largest private investments in the South are by Montedison and they have large petrochemical interests in the Siracusa area, producing fertilizers and a range of chemical products. The area Siracusa–Augusta, which already has this Montedison chemical plant and an oil refinery linked by pipeline to the small oilfield near Ragusa, is being developed with an eye to its geographical endowment. The articulated coast between the two towns facilitates the building of jetties to deep water and offers advantages for port development not found elsewhere in Sicily. Augusta can now accommodate 250 000-ton tankers. Plans now being implemented include a large expansion of oil refining (crude oil being brought in by sea) and petrochemicals output, with emphasis on the production of synthetic resins, plastics, synthetic rubber, and detergents. The cement industry will be enlarged and mechanical engineering is to be introduced, as is the refining of imported non-ferrous ores (Fig. 8). With the other petrochemical industries at Gela near the Ragusa oilfield, eastern Sicily is coming to have one of the main oil refinery and petrochemical complexes in Western Europe. In Sardinia, near Cagliari,

Montedison has reorganized the old lead and zinc workings and nearby at Sulcis-Iglesiente a large alumina plant to treat imported bauxite has been built. In the north of the island at Porto Torres a large petrochemical works was completed in 1970, while in central Sardinia near Ottana the government-controlled E.N.I. and Montedison reluctantly have built a synthetic textile plant of dubious viability, since it is set amid a farming and pastoral community with a lack of both physical and social infrastructure. There seems little prospect of its paying its way for many years.

*　　*　　*

These examples demonstrate the character of much of the industrial development and planning during the late 1960s. Most of the industrial investment was from the public rather than from

Fig. 8. Siracusa-Augusta industrial region planning

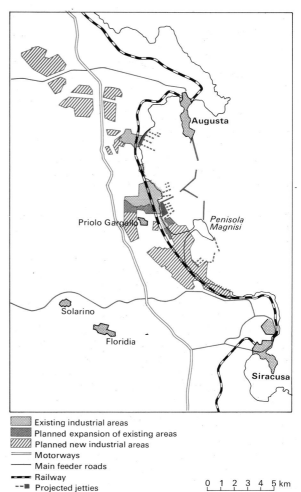

▨ Existing industrial areas
▨ Planned expansion of existing areas
▨ Planned new industrial areas
═ Motorways
— Main feeder roads
▄▄▄ Railway
▄▄▄■ Projected jetties

0 1 2 3 4 5 km

the private sector and the majority of the industries were capital-intensive rather than labour-intensive, leading to greater productivity per worker but not absorbing the large numbers moving out of agriculture. Between 1951 and 1969 a total of 1 095 000 new jobs were provided in the South but 1 700 000 persons emigrated from the South. Except in selected areas, such as Latina (near to Rome) private industry has been wary of the South; it has seen the great plants established by the State-controlled firms and has called them 'cathedrals in the desert'. The lack of industrial tradition and technical know-how among southern labour has been a telling factor in deterring private firms in the North from venturing south and by 1970 some 70 per cent of Italian industry was still to be found in the North (with over 90 per cent of those firms having 500 or more employees). These views are changing but the change takes time. Thus private industry lags behind State-controlled industry in investment and 'take-off' conditions have not yet been achieved. However, twenty years of effort and enormous investments are gradually taking effect. Table 5 shows that the more traditional industries of the South are losing importance to new developments (although in absolute terms their output increased).

The I.R.I.-built autostrade have had the effect of 'shrinking the Italian boot'. Motorways from the North to both 'toe' and 'heel' are now completed and the South is no longer isolated by its poor communications. The motorways themselves attract business, although generally in a strip about twelve kilometres wide each side of the road. The combination of Cassa incentives and high-speed motorway has attracted industry in a ribbon development extending from Rome to Naples, and with the more southerly part now completed it is hoped that this pattern will lengthen southwards. Poor villages exist a few kilometres from the new autostrade, but increasingly the labour from them is attracted to the industries and village incomes start to rise. The establishment in 1970 of regional government was expected to presage increased attempts by the southern regions to attract new private industry to locations where adequate physical and social infrastructure existed. Unfortunately the middle period of the 1970s was one of economic depression in Italy, with factories working at no more than 70 per cent capacity and with 2 million unemployed, most of them being in the South. In this period the decrease in industrial production within the Mezzogiorno was actually less than that of the North, mainly because much southern industry makes traditional products serving essential local demand and there is little manufacture of for example, synthetic fibres and textiles which suffered a large fall in demand. However, the recession hardened the reluctance of private industry to invest in the South, particularly as the fragility of all Italy's industrial sector had been exposed.

In 1976 a new law for the Mezzogiorno was passed which reduced the powers of the Cassa in favour of the semi-autonomous regions, reshaped financial aids and concessions in favour of medium and smaller firms, and earmarked a further £10 000 million for Mezzogiorno development up to 1980.

As the years have passed the Cassa has received much criticism: its costly policies have not yet ensured the economic take-off of the South and many of its 'cathedrals in the desert' are still not viable and have failed to attract the vital halo of supporting industry. The new law confines the Cassa to the operation of special projects of interregional nature and most of its former activities have passed to the regional authorities. The complex system of industrial incentives has been simplified and recast in favour of medium and small enterprises and large companies will no longer be eligible for soft loans. All the earlier incentives particularly helped capital intensive industries, but labour costs in the North and South are now practically equal, so increased assistance to the smaller and more labour intensive enterprises represents a further phase of the continuing attempts to create a more balanced distribution of productive activities between the two areas and to reduce the role of the South as a labour reservoir for the North.

Tourism

There can be no doubt that the future will see an immense development of tourism and holiday-making in the Mezzogiorno. It is indeed astonishing that the region has not yet been 'discovered' by tour and package-holiday operators, and that it is still largely the haunt of the discerning tourist keen to avoid crowded and over-popular resorts. The principal reason for this belated recognition of what could be one of Mediterranean Europe's most renowned holiday areas has been its relative remoteness, now no longer the case since the completion of the fast autostrade right down to the 'toe' and to the 'heel'. No longer need the holiday-maker cease his southerly journey at Naples and the Sorrento Peninsula, there to visit the beautiful but over-commercialized Amalfi, Positano, and Capri. He can be whisked southwards at high speed to take his choice of kilometres of empty sandy beaches and pleasant coves scarcely inhabited except here and there by fishermen and their boats. Calabria could offer lavishly illustrated tours of Mediterranean civilization and history: Greek and Roman ruins, Byzantine churches, Norman fortresses, baroque cathedrals. Inland is every type of scenery from plain to precipitous mountain, from lemon groves to beech forests, from the crowded hilltop village to the Alpine hut. The Adriatic and Ionian coasts offer long silver beaches and shallow waters for safe bathing; the chalk cliffs of the Gargano peninsula, picturesque grottoes; the Salentine peninsula, its Trulli settlements amid vines and almonds; the Metapontino, a sandy coast backed by peach blossom and oranges. Sicily (especially its east coast beneath volcanic Etna and its north coast around Palermo) is already a delight to many, most of whom fly to the island. Yet here also the potential for the tourist industry has scarcely been tapped and so much more than Taormina in its Riviera-like setting and the sophisticated resort of Mondella Beach near Palermo await discovery.

For the epicure the Mezzogiorno offers a wealth of new dishes and variants on established Italian favourites. Aubergines in royal purple splendour gracing the stalls of open-air markets may be enjoyed sliced, fried with cheese and tomato sauce, and stuffed with anchovies and olives. The forms and varieties of pasta and their treatment seem infinite: the hard local wheat and the ever-present tomato combined with cheese form a base, and often sea-food—such as mussels —provide a garnish and sauce. The subtly flavoured *pizza Napoletana* can vie with the strong local salami, and the sea-food dishes all around the coast rival the *bouillabaisse* of Provence: there are meaty fish like swordfish and tunny which provide steaks to grill over charcoal, and smaller anchovies, sardines, eels, varieties of octopus, and numerous molluscs which in a rich sauce become *zuppa alla marinara*.

Naples is the mecca for ice-cream lovers (true ice-cream, not the factory variety) and all over the South the quality and the range of flavours from local fruit juice is unrivalled; among the less usual are lime, peach, apricot, and pistachio. Southern wines, except probably Marsala and Lacrima Christi, have no great international reputation, yet exploring the local wines—the reds generally robust, the whites dry and smooth —is a pleasant and not too expensive occupation. In recent years improvement and standardization of many local wines has come about with the establishment of wine co-operatives under the Enti di Riforma. The South, with all it can offer in sunshine, natural beauty, and native courtesy, deserves to be better known and in time will become widely appreciated.

The Cassa recognizes that tourism has an important part to play in southern development and in recent years substantial funds have been disbursed to further this sector of the economy. Most effort is concentrated into selected Areas of Tourist Development and loans are available for building, enlarging, and modernizing hotels, hostels, and tourist villages. The new main roads to the South are supplemented by many new and resurfaced roads within the South; they are amply provided with petrol stations and, except in limited areas, as yet with little traffic. Here motoring can become a pleasure. Many more hotels are under construction and gradually the amenities sought by most holiday-makers are beginning to appear beside the golden beaches.

To sum up briefly, it is apparent that in the field of industry and tourism the recent decade has seen immense intervention, by the government through its various agencies, to attract and foster a wide range of secondary occupations in order to achieve the diversification that a more efficient agricultural sector needs for its surplus workers. A growth-area policy that will achieve local economic advances and create magnets to migrant rural population has been adopted and put into practice, but so far the region as a whole has not attained the level of expansion that is needed for the 'take-off'. One of the reasons for this is the slowness of private industrial investment—almost half of southern gross industrial investment has come from the State-controlled firms. A further disappointment has been in the limited numbers of small and medium-sized firms establishing in the South and the relatively few that have blossomed from indigenous growth, for in the South there is a dearth of both entrepreneurial and managerial ability. So far much of the main industrial development in the South has been capital-intensive and has not absorbed labour at the rate it has been leaving the land. The new measures being enacted may help to overcome the doubts of private industrialists. In this respect the decade 1975–85 is critical for the Mezzogiorno.

6 Twenty-five Years of Endeavour

If the processes of the last twenty-five years are simplified, it may be said that the economic development of Italy's South follows the standard pattern first of agricultural improvement, and then the siphoning off of surplus agricultural labour into industry and service occupations. A decade was spent on agricultural and infrastructure improvement before the equally necessary expansion of industry was given attention; by the end of the second decade much had been successfully accomplished in agriculture and the pressing need was for more and more industrial and service opportunities to absorb the new entrants into the labour market, and the growing numbers becoming surplus to a more efficient and productive agriculture. This task has not yet been accomplished and therefore is accompanied by unemployment and large-scale migration.

Migration is often cited as a sorry practice which represents a serious loss to the South and which ought to be brought to an end. In a social sense this argument has much to be said for it, but in an economic sense it must be realized that for a long time to come emigration from the South is a very necessary feature in the development of that great region. The development plans for 1965–70 were realistic in this view and despite proposing massive investment in the South so that 40 per cent of the nation's new non-agricultural jobs should be found there, it was estimated that a net migration of 350 000 from South to North would be necessary during the plan-period. This figure is arrived at by assuming that natural increase of workers and reduction of unemployment would require 570 000 new jobs (after allowing for some 200 000 who were likely to emigrate abroad); further, some 350 000 would be moving out of agriculture, making a total of 920 000 seeking non-agricultural employment. The plan could provide jobs for only 570 000; the balance were expected to move North, mainly to the North-west. Migration from the South throughout the last decade averaged about 130 000 a year. To some extent the movement from South to North evens up the rate of natural increase of the population, for the rate in the South at 2·9 per cent is high while that of the North at 1·1 per cent is low. Thus we find, for example, that between 1951 and 1956 the population of the metropolitan area of Greater Milan increased by almost 1·5 million, in-migration accounting for 70 per cent of it. Migration into Greater Turin during that period was responsible for 88 per cent of its increase of 570 000.

Fundamentally, the more who leave southern agriculture, the faster will those remaining on the land be emancipated from subsistence-type farming. A shift of crop patterns from, for example, cereal to dairy or citrus-fruit farming, becomes possible more quickly. This is all part of the process of rendering agriculture more efficient. In terms of migration to the North, then, the movement from the South effectively reduces the rate of population growth there and reduces the 'food gap' (i.e. net food imports into the South), or in effect helps to raise income per head among those remaining and allows that population to consume more and more industrial produce, thus widening the southern market and offering more incentive to industrialization. Thus emigration has a positive part to play in policies for the South and, if this view is held, gives the lie to critics who regard it as a sign that southern policies are proving unsuccessful or that future industrial growth should be kept to the North.

Migration from the Mezzogiorno today bears no relation to that before 1920. The numbers involved are smaller, destinations are mainly to northern Italy and other Common Market countries (making emigration cheaper and easier) and incomes from the South are rising as agricultural improvement continues and increasing opportunities occur in manufacturing and in service industries. Remittances back to the South are valuable income supplements. The disadvantages of emigration include the fact that it is the productive part of the population that is involved (i.e. mainly the young and active) and that they are those with most initiative and potential entrepreneurial talent. In that sense they are a distinct loss to the Mezzogiorno in its present stage of development.

The present heavy emphasis on industrialization represents the attempt to establish an urban society in the South in place of the traditional agricultural one, for industrialization generally equates with urbanization and especially so in the Mezzogiorno where particular regions have been selected as 'growth poles'. Urban values,

The old and the new, a view of the modern potassic salt mine at San Cataldo, Sicily

institutions, and customs are spreading, bringing new ways of life and thought to the South: this is an essential part of the modernization process. The South has too long felt the lack of dynamic and enterprising cities such as one finds in the North. With their growth a more modern outlook, an acceptance of innovation, and adaptability to change will bring the new dimension to southern society that the hesitant industrialists of the North are seeking.

Increasingly the Cassa has been concentrating its assistance into selected areas where fast economic growth is deemed possible: into 82 Agricultural Development Zones, into 29 Areas of Tourist Development and 42 Areas or Nuclei of Industrial Development. Many of these overlap and in five where there is most overlapping, 'growth poles' have been designated. This current policy of Area Development is likely to ensure rapid growth and at lower cost, but will raise social problems as population is attracted into the Areas and urbanization speeds up. Clearly much of the South, outside these areas, no longer

has the prospect of major development effort, but most of this lies in the hilly and mountainous areas where heavy tasks and expenditure on rehabilitation of the terrain are necessary if change is to come. This is one of the less exciting tasks that lies ahead for the Cassa and the new regional governments.

The Mezzogiorno is one of several peripheral problem regions of the European Economic Community. By the Treaty of Rome that body is pledged to a reduction of economic differences between the various regions and to mitigating the backwardness of the less favoured. Actions of the Community such as the establishment of Free Trade within its boundaries give rise to regional problems and may aggravate existing regional inequalities. Thus the Mezzogiorno is not to be regarded solely as Italy's problem. Community agencies which help regional development are still weak, but have made a contribution. The European Investment Bank, established in 1959, has been particularly concerned to help regional development and in its first

45

decade some 58 per cent of its loans went to the Cassa. Other more marginal help has come from the European Agricultural Fund and the European Social Fund. Of particular importance have been specific regional studies carried out by the E.E.C. for the help of member states: in this category comes the valuable study of the Bari–Taranto–Brindisi areas as a possible industrial complex. There is a need for the E.E.C. to play a more forthright part in tackling the Community's regional problems, and this has been acknowledged since the Community was enlarged in 1973.

Twenty-five years may seem a long time, but not for the enormous task the Italian government and Cassa undertook in 1950. This is recognized in the life of the Cassa being repeatedly renewed, now until 1980. Some crude assessments of the success of measures taken is possible, but they can only give a partial picture. For example, net per capita income in the South has been rising faster than that of the North. In 1950 it was only half that of the North, now it is two-thirds, but still far too low for an E.E.C. country. The occupational structure has undergone a remarkable transformation over the twenty years. In 1950 agriculture employed 57 per cent, industry 20 per cent, and services 43 per cent of the occupied population. In 1970 the figures were: agriculture 33 per cent, industry 32 per cent, and services 35 per cent. Many thousands of millions of pounds have been invested in the South over this period and the full effects of this massive investment have yet to be felt. The economic structure of the South is now on a sounder basis: agriculture has shed 1·5 million workers, infrastructure is substantial, illiteracy is lower, overcrowding in housing has fallen by 20 per cent. There is no doubt that since 1950 there has been more advance in the Mezzogiorno than in the whole of the preceding 90 years since Unification: yet a substantial gap between North and South remains. For much of the South poverty is still the unhappy lot of the masses. In Calabria, one of the poorest regions, the average income is only half the national average (and one-third that of the Milanese), infant mortality is twice as high as in the North, and agricultural yields about one-half to one-third less. Emigration from this region is high. Spontaneous development has not yet come to the South but may do so during the 1975–85 decade when the fruits of infrastructure investment may be gathered. So far the emphasis on large-scale basic, heavy industry has taken much capital but not offered a great deal of employment. It is hoped this picture will now change as more medium-scale consumer goods industries move into the South.

Regional policies are being applied in Italy more forcefully than in any other European country. Incentives, preferences, and direct interventions (in place of local entrepreneurship) have become more and more pronounced over the years, crystallizing in growth-area policies following upon infrastructure provision. This is why the progress of the Mezzogiorno is being watched so closely by those concerned with economic development, for every country has its South and North to a greater or lesser degree and formulation of their regional policies may come to owe much to the Italian experience.

TABLE 6

Socio-economic indicators of change 1951–71
Southern Italy's share (%) of Italian total

	1951	1971
Resident population	37·2	34·8
Meat consumption	24·2	30·6
Cigarette consumption	28·0	30·5
Electricity for lighting	20·5	24·5
Number of telephones	10·4	20·6
Number of radio/TV licences	20·6	26·2
Number of motor vehicles	17·7	23·5
Number of beds in hospitals	21·9	26·4
Post Office savings	29·4	37·8

Source: G. Tagliacarne, 'Socio-economic dynamics of the Regions between 1951 and 1971' *Review of Economic Conditions in Italy,* **27**, p. 127 (1973).

Further Work

It is assumed that the student will have a good atlas map of Italy to hand while he reads this book (the Oxford Atlas is recommended).

General geography texts on Italy, which allow the Mezzogiorno to be placed within the national setting, are:

D. S. Walker, *A Geography of Italy*, London (1967).

J. P. Cole, *Italy*, London (1964).

A more advanced volume, although covering a wider area is:

J. M. Houston, *The Western Mediterranean World*, London (1964)

while aspects of the Mezzogiorno population are examined in:

R. E. Dickinson, *The Population Problem of Southern Italy*, Syracuse (1955).

Advanced volumes on the economic aspects of regional planning in southern Italy are:

K. Allen and M. C. MacLennan, *Regional Problems and Policies in Italy and France*, London (1970).

K. Allen and A. Stevenson, *An Introduction to the Italian Economy*, London (1974).

Most recent work on the Mezzogiorno appears in articles in a range of journals; among the geographical ones are:

R. E. Dickinson, 'Land reform in southern Italy', *Economic Geography* (1954).

R. King, 'Structural and geographical problems of south Italian agriculture', *Norsk Geografisk Tidsskrift* (1970).

—— 'Land reform in Apulia-Lucania-Molise', *Norsk Geografisk Tidsskrift* (1970).

—— 'Sardinia's land reform policy', *Geographical Magazine* (March 1970).

—— 'Sicily, Mediterranean island in torment', *Geographical Magazine* (December 1971).

—— 'History and evaluation of agricultural development schemes in Sardinia', *Tidjschrift voor Economische en Sociale Geografie* (1971).

—— 'Ottana: an attempt to bring industry to Sardinia's shepherd-bandits', *Geography* (July 1975).

A. B. Mountjoy, 'Industrial development in Apulia', *Geography* (November 1966).

—— 'Industrial development in Eastern Sicily', *Geography* (November 1970).

—— 'Pressures and progress in southern Italy', *Geographical Magazine* (July 1970).

C. J. Robertson, 'Land utilisation in Calabria', *Geography* (November 1957).

A. Rodgers, 'Naples, a case study of government subsidisation of industrial development', *Tidjschrift voor Economische en Sociale Geografie* (1966).

—— 'Migration and industrial development: the southern Italian experience', *Economic Geography* (1970).

C. D. Smith, 'Mezzogiorno in perspective', *Geographical Magazine* (July 1970).

L. Unger, 'Rural settlement in Campania', *Geographical Review* (1953).

Other sources of information (including statistical) are:

Istituto Centrale di Statistica, *Annuario Statistico Italiano* (Rome).

Review of Economic Conditions in Italy (bimonthly) Banca di Roma, and various reports and brochures obtainable from the Cassa per il Mezzogiorno, Rome.

There is no other problem region in Europe that is a true analogue of the Mezzogiorno, but for comparative purposes the recent planning developments in Andalusia should be examined (see the volume by J. Naylon in this series) and the reasons for similarities and dissimilarities should be analysed.

Most of the tables included in the text are susceptible to further analysis and to graphical and cartographical presentation. This is recommended for a fuller understanding of the relationships which the figures demonstrate.

Index